Praise for *Anatomy of a* [...]

"Guiding us to the seed of witchcraft, Laura has skillfully prepared a beautiful garden to grow our magical bodies in. *Anatomy of a Witch* does a masterful job of bringing us back to the roots of our practice with fun and practical techniques, all while reminding us that we are made of more than just flesh and blood, and that our bodies are often the best tools we need to be magical people."

—Dana Newkirk, costar of *Hellier* and head curator
of the Traveling Museum of the Paranormal & Occult

"In *Anatomy of a Witch*, Laura has illuminated a topic that has begged explanation for many years. Using a full array of tools—tarot, sigil magic, journaling, knowledge lectures and ritual—Laura takes the Witch on a journey that leads to full body acceptance and a deep encounter with both the physical and spiritual bodies. A wonderful interplay of wit and profound knowledge act as guideposts for a journey that every aspiring adept should take."

—Andrew Theitic, publisher of *The Witches' Almanac, LTD*

"The deepest experience you can have with Witchcraft is connected to embodiment. There is no better guide to embodying Witchcraft than *Anatomy of a Witch* by Laura Tempest Zakroff. From breathwork, to acknowledging your body as sacred space, to feeling into your sacred physical centers, this book will bring your Witchcraft practice to the next level. Tempest shares this work in a conversational style that makes you feel like you are hanging out with her."

—Phoenix LeFae, author of *Walking in Beauty* and *What Is Remembered Lives*

"In this book, Laura Tempest Zakroff reacquaints readers with their bodies, reconnecting them with breath, blood, bone, and that sacred temple through which we both experience and act in the world. Through exercises involving images from the tarot, sigils, everyday rituals, daily practice, and movement, readers will rediscover their Witchy bodies and the magic that flows through them and permeates the world around them."

—Sabina Magliocco, author of *Witching Culture* and professor of anthropology
at the University of British Columbia, Vancouver

"Laura Tempest Zakroff fills an important gap in what can often be a very heady and overly mentally focused practice by anchoring it into the vehicle which we actually do all of our magic with: the human body. A clear and (most importantly) useful book filled with exercises and practices to deepen the readers connection to their physical being."

—Aidan Wachter, author *of Six Ways: Approaches &*
Entries for Practical Magic and *Weaving Fate*

"Zakroff guides Witches of all paths in working with the most indispensable tool available to them: the self. Though this book is about the body, and the energetic portals and magick available through this, what it's really about is living a soul-centered and magick-centered life, rooted in the intelligence of the flesh."

—Gabriela Herstik, author of *Inner Witch*, *Bewitching*
the Elements, and *Embody Your Magick*

"Laura Tempest Zakroff, in her masterful style, does a brilliant job of taking the ethereal life of the Witch and bringing it into the sacred, grounded body of anatomy. This book is a fantastic read for anyone seeking new levels of communication with their Witch body as a whole, complete system of magick."

—Najah Lightfoot, author of *Good Juju*

"*Anatomy of a Witch* deftly weaves together ideas, reflections, and practical exercises that deepen and expand your connection to the greatest of spiritual vessels, your body. If you would like to more fully become your magick made manifest, then read this book and do the work that it offers."

—Ivo Dominguez Jr., author of *The Four Elements of the Wise*

"This book is a resource, an affirmation, and a gift. Every subsequent page settles me further into what I've always felt to be true, that my own heart and mind and hands are the most powerful magical tools I could ever have. With *Anatomy of a Witch*, Tempest has given me, given us, space to breathe and dance again, and to know unshakably that we, ourselves, are in fact the real deal."

—S. J. Tucker, musician & magical practitioner

Anatomy
of a
Witch

About the Author

Laura Tempest Zakroff is a professional artist, author, dancer, designer, and Modern Traditional Witch based in New England. She holds a BFA from the Rhode Island School of Design and her artwork has received awards and honors worldwide. Her work embodies myth and the esoteric through her drawings and paintings, jewelry, talismans, and other designs. Laura is the author of the bestselling Llewellyn books *Weave the Liminal: Living Modern Traditional Witchcraft* and *Sigil Witchery: A Witch's Guide to Crafting Magick Symbols*, as well as the *Liminal Spirits Oracle* (artist/author), *The Witch's Cauldron*, and *The Witch's Altar* (co-authored with Jason Mankey). Laura edited *The New Aradia: A Witch's Handbook to Magical Resistance* (Revelore Press). She blogs for Patheos as *A Modern Traditional Witch*, contributes to *The Witches' Almanac, Ltd.*, and creates the *Witchual Workout* and other programming on her YouTube channel. Laura is the creative force behind several community events and teaches workshops worldwide. Find out more at www.LauraTempestZakroff.com.

Anatomy of a Witch

a Map to the Magical Body

Laura Tempest Zakroff

author of *WEAVE THE LIMINAL*

Foreword by Christopher Penczak

Llewellyn Publications · Woodbury, Minnesota

FIRST EDITION
Third Printing, 2022

Cover art by Laura Tempest Zakroff
Cover design by Shira Atakpu
Interior art by Laura Tempest Zakroff

Llewellyn Publications is a registered trademark of Llewellyn Worldwide Ltd.

Library of Congress Cataloging-in-Publication Data
Names: Zakroff, Laura Tempest, author.
Title: Anatomy of a witch : a map to the magical body / by Laura Tempest
  Zakroff.
Description: First edition. | Woodbury, Minnesota : Llewellyn Worldwide,
  [2021] | Includes bibliographical references. | Summary: "This is a book
  for Witches to connect with their bodies and the living world around
  them. It can be used by any Witch or Pagan looking for a more grounded
  connection between magic and their body"— Provided by publisher.
Identifiers: LCCN 2021005644 (print) | LCCN 2021005645 (ebook) | ISBN
  9780738764344 (paperback) | ISBN 9780738764580 (ebook)
Subjects: LCSH: Witchcraft. | Magic. | Mind and body.
Classification: LCC BF1566 .Z35 2021 (print) | LCC BF1566 (ebook) | DDC
  133.4/3—dc23
LC record available at https://lccn.loc.gov/2021005644
LC ebook record available at https://lccn.loc.gov/2021005645

Llewellyn Worldwide Ltd. does not participate in, endorse, or have any authority or responsibility concerning private business transactions between our authors and the public.

All mail addressed to the author is forwarded but the publisher cannot, unless specifically instructed by the author, give out an address or phone number.

Any internet references contained in this work are current at publication time, but the publisher cannot guarantee that a specific location will continue to be maintained. Please refer to the publisher's website for links to authors' websites and other sources.

Llewellyn Publications
A Division of Llewellyn Worldwide Ltd.
2143 Wooddale Drive
Woodbury, MN 55125-2989
www.llewellyn.com

Printed in the United States of America

Other Works by Laura Tempest Zakroff

Books & Oracles

Liminal Spirits Oracle

(Llewellyn, 2020)

Weave the Liminal: Living Modern Traditional Witchcraft

(Llewellyn, 2019)

Sigil Witchery

(Llewellyn, 2018)

The Witch's Altar (with Jason Mankey)

(Llewellyn, 2018)

The Witch's Cauldron

(Llewellyn, 2017)

The New Aradia: A Witch's Handbook to Magical Resistance

(Editor, Revelore, 2018)

Coloring Books

Myth & Magick (2016)

The Art of Bellydance (2016)

Witch's Brew (2016)

Steampunk Menagerie (2015)

Instructional DVDs

DecoDance (2015)

Bellydance Artistry (2011)

Forthcoming Works

Anatomy of a Witch Oracle

(Llewellyn, 2022)

For all those who move in mysterious ways,
(and) in loving memory of Sam

Contents

Chapter 3: The Serpent   67

Chapter 4: Witch Bones   87

Illustrations

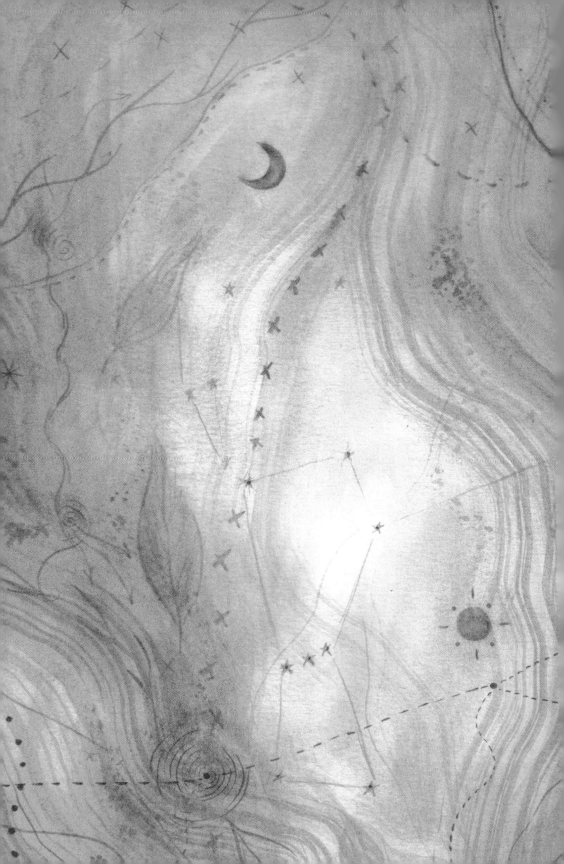

Rituals, Witchuals & Other Exercises

Foreword
by Christopher Penczak

In the modern magickal classic *The Sandman* by Neil Gaiman, one of the characters, Lyta, goes on a quest to seek aid from the Furies, the Greek goddesses who mete out justice and vengeance. She asks them, "Are you…are you the Furies?"

And they respond, "Are we the Furies? Are you a hand? Or an eye? Or a tooth?"

Lyta says, "No, of course not. I am myself. But I have those things within me…"

That simple exchange embodies such deep magickal wisdom for us all. Here Gaiman speaks to the nature of how we, and the gods, are many things, many identities and roles within something larger, and uses the very tangible parts of the body to illustrate the less tangible divinities within us. We are all made up of many parts. We have many things inside us, and by exploring those things within, we can better embody ourselves. They lead to that essential "myself."

Witches continue to seek their essential self today, as they have done since the very beginning, but an area often neglected by today's Witches are the very tangible parts of ourselves, those parts within our body, our very organs and structures, and the magickal forces found in all people, deeply anchored in the parts of our body. Just as the hand, eye, and tooth contain wisdom for us, Laura Tempest Zakroff takes us on a magickal journey through our own bodies, drawing a fivefold pentacle teaching us through the lungs, heart, serpent, bones, and mind.

Our bodies are the crossroads between our consciousness and our experience. Our physical senses are the primary interface for our experiences in the world. Witchcraft is an Art as much as it is anything else, but it is an embodied art. Life is the medium for our Art, and that life is the intersection of our consciousness and body with the world around us, physical and non-physical. So much traditional Witchcraft and occultism is visceral and sensory to hone our awareness of this sensory interface. We must feel Witchcraft on all levels to truly and deeply practice it. It's in our minds, yes, one of the five points of these teachings, but it is also down to our very bones. Some, including myself, focus so much on the visionary, the otherworldly, and the mystical that we lose sight of the magick in our blood and bones, in our breath and dance, in sweat, and tears, in pleasure and in pain. Many are enamored with Witchcraft and magick as an escape from the world and the body, yet true Witchcraft is anything but escapism. Witchcraft is facing what is to make what could be possible. Laura doesn't shy away from this, telling us outright that while the body is amazing, it is also messy and sometimes awful, with its surprises and challenges. If you are looking for a clean, pristine path without any mess, you are in for some surprises when you walk the Witch's path.

The body moves us in the worlds both seen and unseen. The senses, physical and psychic, help us navigate and commune with these worlds. The body of the Witch, and in fact any body, identified as Witch or not, is both the map and the terrain. One of the classic occult teachings known as the Principle of Correspondence tells us on the most cosmic level, "As above, so below," and in quoting it, most people forget the second part, "As within, so without." It's not just a maxim of astrology, but how the outside world and experience we can see corresponds to what is going on within us. Most relegate that to the psychological, what we are thinking and feeling, but it is also a literal teaching. Our organs, blood, and bones are within, as well as our thoughts and emotions. When we change our breath, our movement, our heart rate, our body chemistry, we change the world without, or at least our experience of it.

This Principle of Correspondence can be found in the old myths of the creation of the universe. There are many types of creation stories, with similarities cutting across cultures, languages, times, and places, but one that often comes up is the concept of the cosmic body. The universe is literally the body of a divine being. Some Witchcraft traditions see it as the Star Goddess. Other traditions look to the creation of the world as the sacrifice of the cosmic body, the first or largest divinity. We see it in the Norse tradition of Ymir, the giant, and in the Sumerian tradition of the serpent dragon Tiamat. The body is sacrificed and the next generation of gods makes the world we know from the body. Bones become mountains. Blood becomes rivers and seas. The skull becomes the vault of heaven.

While I favor a model of a living cosmos where we are all cells within a living body, not one made from a corpse, across both of these myths, living and dead, is embedded the reason for sacred proportions, geometries, and correspondences between our own bodies and the body of the cosmos. We are all living things made in the same patterns and shapes. Looking to one, we learn about the others, be it the stars or our own body processes, cycles, and structures. They are all divine. While we can feel separate from nature, the body itself is the map of the cosmos. So we should probably get more familiar with it if we seek to experience the cosmic mysteries. We can start with our breath. We can start with our blood. We can dig deep into our bones. From these three, we find the more ephemeral serpentine powers of primal life force, so deeply tied with the iconography of the Witch, and we can more clearly understand the powers of the mind, not just residing in the brain but permeating our entire body through the nervous system and beyond.

I can think of no better guide than Laura Tempest Zakroff on the path of the embodied Witch, exploring the cosmos within and without. She expertly mixes intellectual knowledge, firsthand experience, sensitivity to our uniqueness in body and soul, poetic truth, and specific instructions. She can draw upon the imagery of pop-culture wisdom to make her point, such as the writings of Terry Pratchett or the lions of Voltron pointing to a deeper alchemical truth, and bring you to a place where you can experience it yourself. So make sure you do. This book can be messy. It's not just something to read and then put down. *Anatomy of a Witch* is a book of doing; otherwise you missed the point of the book and really the entire point of Witchcraft. Witchcraft is taking in with our body, with our senses. Witchcraft is found in the doing, and the body is our vessel for doing. Most importantly, Witchcraft is being. We are Witches and we simply are, radiating our being into the world. The body is our physical point of manifestation in this world. We exist in the body, with all that entails. Here we learn to go deeper in understanding just what the body entails, to be the Witch.

Christopher Penczak
Co-founder of the Temple of Witchcraft

Introduction

The Witch's body is
a constellation of stars,
eyes that pierce the darkness,
lips that speak in song and silence,
ears attuned to the voices of spirits,
lungs that breathe the liminal,
a heart of fire pulsing an ecstatic dance,
hips full of serpent wisdom,
fingers that weave the mysteries,
and feet that kiss the earth.

Imagine that you are a constellation—a cosmic being made up of stars. You contain swirling galaxies made up of orbiting planets and many moons. Your body seems endless, hinting at untold depths and buzzing with the secret songs of space. You are both visible and invisible: made up of both what can be seen by the naked eye and the unknown mysteries that inspire the imaginations of others. Myths are told and retold of your epic journeys. Countless people are guided by your path across the sky through the seasons. To them, your celestial body is a map to navigate not only the physical world but the mysteries of the universe as well.

Sounds pretty magical and amazing, right? Well, the body you reside in right this minute is just as magical and amazing. Not only do you have in your possession the physical marvel that is the living human body, but you also have the anatomy of a Witch. Your body is a living map, made of star stuff and ready to direct and guide your journey.

The human body is a vessel for magic, but it is more than just some container; the body is multifaceted and a miraculous residence. If you follow down a serpentine path of blood, breath, and bone—intermingled with elements—the Witch's body can be found and known. In the space between bones and muscles, nerves and blood vessels, flows the capacity for magic—a spirit being dwelling in flesh. That spirit is you. The body is a conduit for bringing fleshly and metaphysical worlds together.

The Witch is flesh.
The Witch is thought.
The Witch is spirit.

A Witch knows they are connected to and a part of the world around them, both what is seen and unseen. Witches tap into universal rhythms, following the beat of their heart to find their way. The Witch listens to the primal self within, striking a balance between action and rest. Traditions of the past provide a structure for the Witch to build a living practice upon. Lastly, a Witch is guided by wisdom that pulls from the mysterious and metaphysical, along with the practical and profound.

One of the things that Witches do best is weave liminal threads, connecting realms and spirits in their work. But understanding how to develop these skills goes beyond reading a book or being told what it's like. The way to truly experience Witchcraft is to learn to embody it. Mysteries have to be experienced in order to be revealed and understood. The path is akin to walking a labyrinth—a process to get to the center and spiral back out again—a pilgrimage to the inner workings of the self. The journey must begin with the body, taking metaphysical and physical steps alike.

The challenge of today's Witch is to fully embrace our body and tap into our personal power, despite whatever constructs and limitations society may seek to place upon us. Through those lived experiences, we gain the wisdom to connect with the seen and unseen worlds, as well as each other. We become truly ourselves—capable, present, and powerful.

Discovering the Magical Body

So how exactly can you learn to embody your magic and unlock the power and potential within you? This book is an invitation to go on a journey of self-examination and magical exploration. Prepare to look at Witchcraft and your body in ways you have likely never considered before.

While the human body itself has numerous systems and organs—which we can certainly correlate to magical practices in their own way—the body of the Witch will be examined in five metaphorical parts: lungs, heart, serpent, bones, and mind. Together they encapsulate the symbolic essence that directs the Witch's path.

1. Beginning with **Witch Lungs,** we will explore breath as a means for interconnectivity, establishing personal presence, and perceiving invisible influences.

2. The **Witch Heart** provides a rhythm for us to move to as we seek balance within ourselves and with the world around us. The pulse of our blood feeds into ritual, which helps us to communicate and find purpose in our work.

3. Calling upon the most primal part of ourselves, the **Serpent** guides us to strengthen our powers of intuition and protection. As we trace its spiraling path, we discover the healing mysteries of creativity and transformation.

4. **Witch Bones** give us strength and structure to build our practice with. They hold the whispers of our ancestors and the mysteries of death, yet speak of the future as well.

5. The **Weaver,** or Witch Mind, is the creative cauldron that stirs everything together. The purposeful weaver, it remembers, guides, and initiates that spark that directs our path.

This book is a manual to the most magical tool in your possession: your body. Witchcraft is immediate and all around us, and you can more deeply connect with it if you are more powerfully present in your body. We will use the biological systems of the human body as a metaphorical map and elemental guide to explore ritual, work magic, build skills for practical living, and truly experience Witchcraft embodied. The techniques may seem simple, but you will find they are surprisingly powerful. By engaging your body more fully as a primary metaphysical tool, you will find that magic flows so much more smoothly and effectively.

A Witch Is More Than Parts and Pieces

What makes a Witch truly a Witch? Is it how you dress, the words you say, the tools you use, the beauty of your altar, or the size of your library? These things may hint at a witchy life, but they do not define or make the Witch.

Furthermore, being a Witch is not determined by your age, background, whether or not you work with gods, or what's in (or not in) your pants. The Witch has many forms—all ages, shapes, genders, sexualities, and colors. Magic exists outside the limitations of all those boundaries.

The anatomy of the Witch is far more esoteric and yet so much more pervasive and present than basic material associations. Like the many threads of a tapestry, the measure and make of the Witch is found more subtly in the layers of being, doing, feeling, building, and knowing. Look closely and you'll see individual colors and fibers intricately intertwining. Move a little further back and you will start to notice motifs and patterns forming. With a few more steps, shape and color blend—giving way to depth, perspective, and glimpses of larger symbols forming a narrative.

To uncover the anatomy of a Witch, you need to adjust your vision to look at those symbols and the underlying threads that make them up. Symbols have long been used by humanity as a way to simplify a complex idea. They represent something more profound than their surface design implies, often pointing to a hidden meaning or story steeped in metaphor. Metaphors are symbols that form pictures from words and concepts, giving birth to myth and folklore. As you examine and gather up the threads in hand, you will begin to understand how magic can be embodied. You will weave your own myths.

Fivefold Form and the Tarot

There are five main parts that make up the anatomy of the Witch: Lungs, Heart, Serpent, Bones, and Mind. The number 5 has a lot of magical symbolism associated with it. The iconic pentagram, with its five points, not only symbolizes protection and power but also represents the elements of Air, Fire, Water, and Earth combined with Spirit. The figure of the five-pointed star is also a wonderful stand-in for the human body—with a head, arms, and legs. Our hands, with their five digits, are one of the earliest fivefold symbols, ranging from a mark of identity to a means of protection, blessing, and fertility, as well as assistance and directional aid. Five is certainly a number that keeps bringing us back to our bodies.

Symbol has an amazing way of revealing mysteries situated in the everyday and the familiar. Those details and patterns that we might otherwise overlook or take for granted can become visible. This insight is where divinatory systems such as the tarot can come in particularly handy. Divination not only helps us to see more clearly into our future, but also provides a look into the past, and even the present as well. Tarot especially taps into the journey of the human experience, making it very relatable for many people. There are fivefold connections present in the tarot as well. The structure of the tarot has five sections: the four suits in the minor arcana (wands, cups, swords, and pentacles—each correlating to an element) and the major arcana (representing the journey of the self or spirit). Within the minor arcana, the fives represent cycles that require a shift to initiate change. The power of cycle, change, and the opportunity for growth are important motifs to keep in mind. As we explore the magical body, the symbolism of the tarot will accompany us on our journey to deepen our understanding along the way.

Elemental Considerations

In each section, we will be using the elements of Air, Fire, Water, Earth, and Spirit as a guide as well. Each system has a defining element, but that does not mean it is strictly within the realm of only that element. Keep in mind: all of the elements are present in our bodies. We breathe air; our blood, flesh, and bones are made up of Water and Earth; and our metabolic processes and nerve pulses fall under the realm of Fire. Consider the elements to be symbols in the map legend that help orient you in your exploration of the magical body.

Resist getting mentally bogged down with the elements as a means to identity or seeing them in very rigid terms. What do I mean by that? When deciding who calls upon a direction and element in a group circle, have you ever heard or been the one to say, "Well, I'm an X sign, so I should call upon X element." There may be an affinity for that element, but in the end, a person can work with any element successfully, regardless of their sign. Astrologically speaking, someone with Taurus as their Sun sign is not simply just "an Earth sign." There are a multitude of other alliances and correlations—perhaps their rising sign is Leo (Fire) and their Moon is in Gemini (Air). These factors describe us in many ways, but they do not express the entirety of who we are or what we are capable of.

From a physical perspective, I prefer to look at elemental progression in terms of basic science mixed with a bit of magical mythology. In order for the other elements to be active in this realm, Air must first be present. Fire requires the presence of oxygen in order to burn. Water is the result of hydrogen and oxygen molecules combining, and its state is dependent on temperature (steam, liquid, or solid). Earth cannot bring forth life without the other elements to assist. Spirit is the unifying presence between and throughout. As for whether Spirit comes first or last, the answer is yes. Spirit is the essence of energy that makes up the elements, but when Earth, Air, Fire, and Water are combined, there becomes another level of consciousness as well. I like to call this the Voltron factor.[1] Each is whole, powerful, and distinct on its own; but once they are brought together in a common form, they become a unique, multi-level entity or presence.

In his lecture at the Temple of Witchcraft in Salem, New Hampshire, on November 18, 2019, Ivo Dominguez Jr. said: "The Elements are a scale or inter-

---

1. *Voltron* is an animated show spanning several decades and with many adaptations where the story centers around five robotic spaceship lions (that have a subtle consciousness of their own) that are piloted by five humanoids. The lions can combine to form a giant magical robot known as Voltron, the legendary defender of the universe.

face for the underlying principles of the Universe. Effective magick uses symbols, placeholders, frameworks, resonant links, and the flexibility of the human psyche to engage with powers that are vaster than humanity and with those that lie hidden within." I absolutely agree and feel that understanding how the elements work and influence us at a fundamental and natural level enhances the practice of the Witch.

Cardinal—creating/manifesting
Fixed—balancing/maintaining
Mutable—transforming/transitioning

Every element also has cardinal, fixed, and mutable roles or facets to it. An element can energetically be in a creative or manifesting state (cardinal), aiding in maintaining or balancing (fixed), or initiating transformation or transition into another phase (mutable). That means that every element is fluid in what it can do. Every element can bring forth life, and it can usher us into the next one. For example, Air can be the life-giving first breath or the continual exchange of gases between plants and animals, and it can also be a tornado that destroys everything in its path. Each element has what we consider beneficial or creative aspects to it, as well as adverse or destructive effects, but it is solely our perspective that gives them a "good" or "bad" interpretation. We are looking at the essence of nature—which is neither positive nor negative in any sort of moral or ethical sense, but simply is. Being mindful of these varying energies will prevent you from having a limited interpretation of an element.

Body Realism

This book is designed to be a guide to the anatomy of a Witch, as well as the care and maintenance of those bodies on multiple levels. It's a metaphysical owner's manual, if you will, complete with a couple of inspiring diagrams—because pictures!

I would like to make it clear though that I'm not going to be espousing some sanctimonious belief that because the body is sacred, it is somehow perfect or without its problems. The reality is obvious: the body is a messy place. Yes, the human body is truly amazing, but it's also awful and confounding at times too. There are surprise liquids, weird smells, mysterious pains, and chemical imbalances, and age brings all sorts of new and interesting challenges. Bodies malfunction, make bumps and burps, take cuts and bruises, and also grow hair out of the strangest places. They come in all shapes, colors, sizes, abilities, and even configurations. It helps to have a sense of humor about it all and embrace the body's weird charms. In addition to understanding the symbolic parts of the Witch's anatomy, I would like you to feel as comfortable as possible in the physical body you have right now. Regardless of whether you see yourself as messy or meticulous, attractive or average, flailing or functioning, I want you to embrace a certain kind of body positivity for the duration of this book.

Academically, body positivity is the idea that human beings should advocate for the acceptance of all bodies regardless of their form, size, or appearance and challenge social constructs that negate that belief. That is a wonderful thing, but for this book, we're going to give body positivity a little twist. Basically, I'm fairly positive that if you're reading this right now, you have a body. (otherwise congratulations to you on reaching a new quantum state of being!). No matter what your body looks like or how it feels, the fact that it exists *with you in it* is an amazing thing. From the inside out—blood, guts, nocturnal secretions, and all—it's yours for the journey. Acknowledging the presence of your body and its potential power physically and metaphysically is the first step.

On the physical level, this book takes your body and its anatomical systems—yes, some of those ones you learned about in grade school—and interweaves them with the five symbolic systems of the Witch's Lungs, Heart, Serpent, Bones, and Mind. Using the familiar form and function of the biological systems as a foundation, we'll dive into the liminal place that bridges symbolic and mythical essence with physical, practical application. As we go through each section, consider the deeper symbolic meaning behind that anatomy and how this different perspective can enhance your Witchcraft experience.

Even though we'll focus on a different area in each chapter, keep in mind that everything is interconnected. All of the anatomical systems are interwoven at the cellular level. Yes, the heart is the center of the circulatory system, but it also plays a vital part in the endocrine system. Our bones provide the framework and structure for our body, but they also make the blood cells that flow through our veins. Our bodies are communities full of diverse organs working together, every part integral to healthy living (though we can make do without some of them if we must). While it makes sense to examine each system in turn, keep in mind that together they form a whole magical body.

Be open to symbolism as you learn about each system, not only in what is described for each but also what you may discover about yourself along the way. There's always room for more interpretation as well, since you are uniquely you, with your own past experiences as an influence. I can't emphasize enough how important it is to hold space for fluidity of concept as you work with each idea. This book is a metaphorical map to the magical body, but that doesn't mean that there's no off-roading allowed or that you can't trailblaze if you're inspired. Or you might run into some unexpected emotional traffic and need to take a break or find an alternative route. Take your time. Remember, a map gives you the lay of the land, but it's up to you to decide how and when you want to cover that territory. I recommend having an adventurous spirit and perhaps packing a few snacks for the trip.

Also remember, while you are diving deep into metaphor and symbolism, that your body is right here with you—tactile and present. What better way to embody magic than to actually *feel* it? Connecting and interacting with these systems and organs on a physical level also enables us to engage in sympathetic magic. The microcosm can affect the macrocosm; the part can alter the whole. What we did physically can affect us emotionally and spiritually. The mystical aspects of Witchcraft rely on recognizing these connections. What we dismiss as mundane or ordinary is a lost opportunity to influence ourselves and the world around us. Open your mind and body to the potential of the real effects.

Better Than Basic

In every section you will find techniques and practices to assist you along the way. From circle-casting to daily cleansing and protection, sigils, spells, charms, meditations, and more, all are crafted from the perspective of Modern Traditional Witchcraft. This approach means referencing the folklore, myths, and proven traditions of the past while balancing them with modern inspiration and practicality. Witchcraft is a living, breathing practice. Wisdom is found not only in learning about and honoring what has been done before, but also in allowing room for new growth and exploration. To aid you in this process, throughout this book you'll also find "witchuals"—witchy ritual prompts designed to engage your creativity.

Please note that while some people may consider some of the included activities "basic," I am firmly of the belief that:

1. Basics are fundamental to your practice as a Witch. Having a solid foundation is key to building a healthy path.

2. Often people may say they already know how to do a particular thing (like casting a circle), but they rarely know the *why* behind the how. Practicing effective Witchcraft involves knowing both how something is done and why we do it. If you truly understand the why, then you're able to personalize it and find deeper meaning.

3. Seeing how other people approach things can greatly inform and expand how you work. There is always a new way of looking at a common problem or concept. Just because something works doesn't mean it's always the best solution for that particular problem.

4. If you feel you know everything, you have learned nothing. There is always something to learn, and sometimes the practices that appear to be the simplest are technically the most difficult to master.

The activities in this book are designed to be accessible—no expensive tools, supplies, or hard-to-get herbs required. Listen to your body and adjust the activities as needed to suit your ability and comfort level. As you incorporate them into your regular practice, the individual focus areas will continue to reveal themselves to you, while offering you an ever-deepening understanding of your own magical body. Remember that the practice of a Witch is developed through establishing familiarity, building working patterns, and accumulating experience over time.

Lastly keep in mind what you hold in your hands isn't meant to be a book of spells: it's a map for living and breathing magic for the modern Witch. Where that map will take you is strictly up to you. Enjoy the journey!

Enter the Fool: Begin Again
A choice is offered.

As Witches, we enter this world twice. The first time is when we take up residence in our physical body. In that moment, we shift from a noncorporeal existence to an incarnate one, largely bound to the laws of this reality. Born of that merger of spirit and flesh, we find that the world is a place of infinite possibilities. It is ours to touch, taste, smell, hear, see, and explore. Our potential seems limitless—if we can break the binds of culturally applied expectations and restrictions regarding class, gender, sexuality, race, ability, age, and religion.

But before we begin to navigate those challenges, we are the Fool in the tarot, with our next step leading us off a precipice into a new existence ruled by matter. I don't think we enter this world blindly or without forethought, like literally falling off a cliff by accident. I think that instead we sidle up to the diving board, tiptoe to the end, gaze at the dazzling surface below, take a breath, leap, and splash into this reality.

We do not come unprepared or alone either. The Fool may travel light, but tools have been packed for the journey ahead. Perhaps contained within that bundle is the wisdom of past lives to act as a compass with a map for the future. We are joined by the Universe above us and many companions along the way. The Fool's number is 0 (zero), which not only represents a new beginning numerically but also has a shape that is representative of an egg. The egg symbolizes hope, potential, and the continuous cycle of life. Once we crack that shell, a new life has begun again.

The second threshold is passed when we recognize ourselves as Witches. Some people debate whether you can be born a Witch or you need to be made a Witch through initiation of some kind. The answer is yes: you can have the tendencies and skills *and* you can have a title bestowed upon you. But the crucial moment is when you recognize yourself as a Witch. Once again, we are the Fool setting ourselves upon the path to discover just exactly what that means for us. The world takes on a new perspective as we revisit our senses and experiences and embrace our ability to create magic; to be change and to embody it.

Regardless of whether you currently believe that either option involves a choice, consider this: what we do from each moment forward is a series of interwoven choices. Every thread selected adds another detail to the pattern of life. Once you begin the tapestry, you become a vital motif within it, as well as an active weaver.

I believe both thresholds are crossed by choice. We have a choice to enter this world, and we can choose to follow the path of the Witch. You can be "into this weird stuff" or maybe just find it interesting, without taking a more active role besides occasionally dabbling with spells or cards. Those things don't really make a Witch. But once you truly walk on this path, the way you see the world changes. You begin to notice what others overlook, seeing the unseen. The odd becomes familiar, and the once-familiar becomes grounds for new exploration. Most importantly, the way you see *you* changes.

You've made the choice. It is time to climb up that ladder. Feel the wind on your skin and the sun at your back as you survey the world. Take a breath and dive in. Begin anew.

Chapter 1
Witch Lungs

Inhale scent of root, bud, leaf, and vine,
Awaken spirit within divine.
Every breath drawn brings outside within,
Each exhaled speaks of who we have been.
Spell-word spoken, endless circles cast,
Liminal threads of future to past.

Breathe in, breathe out. With every breath, you bring the outside world inside of you. With every exhalation, you share molecules of yourself with the world. Our breath intermingles with others', fueling other life forms, just as their output enables our own lives.

Witch Lungs contain the wisdom of understanding what is permeable and shared and what should be contained and protected. The space that the Lungs encompass is the gateway to invisible worlds and a passport to the divine self.

A Witch knows that they are not only connected to the world around them but also a part of it—both what is seen and unseen. We are immersed in invisible connections and interactions between us, spirits, deities, and the universe. The Witch exudes sovereignty, knowing where they end and the next thread begins.

The Magician

Assembled and present at the altar.

If we study the cards of the major arcana in sequential numerical order, beginning with the Fool at 0, we trace the journey of the embodied spirit through life. Moving to 1 with the Magician, we find the Fool spirit has taken the leap into the physical world and is now firmly ensconced in a body. Just a quick look at the position and posture of the Magician affirms this fact. The Magician is facing forward, which symbolizes being oriented in the present. One arm points up and the other gestures below, connecting the ethereal planes with the physical ones.

The Magician stands behind an altar—a place of sacred action and connection—ready to begin. The tools the Fool carried are now displayed on the altar, their potential waiting to be explored. From here begins the process of learning to understand the rules and reasons of this new existence. Building familiarity with these tools and lessons brings the essence of individuality and the opportunities to create and manifest.

As the Magician, we too have arrived at the altar. We will uncover the power of our greater connection with the world and our individuality. The invisible will become tangible, and we will learn how to own our space. Creativity, manifestation, and possibilities rest just at our fingertips.

The action is ours to initiate. It starts with a simple breath that in turn feeds a forest.

What Are Witch Lungs?

At birth, the first gasp of air officially marks our arrival into this world. That extraordinary breath is often accompanied by a cry, making our presence audibly known. From that moment on, our lungs become a place of exchange between our body and the outside world.

Our lungs are responsible for bringing fresh air into our body, filtering that air into our bloodstream while also releasing waste gases. They enable us to speak, to smell, and to regulate our systems. Lungs are also one of the easiest internal organs for us to sense if we focus our attention on our respiratory system. We can feel the air enter our body through our nasal passages and travel down into our chest. There is the visual evidence of our chest expanding as our lungs take in air—and relaxing as we exhale.

Recognizing what our physical lungs do for us builds the foundation for understanding the Witch Lungs. But we must go beyond the task of filtering oxygen and consider air, breath, space, spirit, and existence in a magical sense.

Witch Lungs teach us the following:

- Everything and everyone is interconnected on some level. We are constantly shifting and exchanging connections—particles, ideas, energy, essence.
- Unseen does not equal unknown. Just because something may seem invisible does not mean it doesn't exist or can't affect, influence, or interact with us. Perception is possible. Embrace the tiny, invisible things that are vastly vital and crucial to fully living.
- There are interior and exterior spaces—those that are personal and public, permeable and protected.
- We must own our breath, recognizing our own sovereignty and power. There is a balance between what we take from the world and what we put into it.

The wisdom found in each of these revelations becomes a key to unlocking more doors within the magical body of the Witch. Grab a suitable key chain (maybe with a nice witchy charm) and let's start collecting those keys.

The Influential Invisible

Life begins with breath. We see breath as the presence of life: we take our first breath as we leave the womb, and give our last breath as we cross over into death. Breath reminds us that there are invisible forces at work that function outside the need for belief or absolute understanding.

We can't see air itself, but we can perceive the effects of it all around us. Stare up at the sky on any day and you will observe clouds in motion, moving across the sky and changing formation at the whims of the wind. Look around you outside and you'll likely see the grass waving in ripples and tree leaves rustling as the breezes run through them. Walk in the city on a cool day and you might glimpse steam vapors rising up from vents that lead to a rumbling subway system. Despite the unseen nature of air, we know that it exists—that it is part of how we live and affects the world around us. The invisible can be seen at work in moving the visible.

Similar to air, magic is generally an unseen force, yet Witches and other magical practitioners know that magic has very real effects on and in the tangible, physical world. Magic happens in the liminal space between the threads that bring us together. Yet we often have such a hard time believing in magic and our own ability to affect the world around us. We are prone to dismissing things as coincidence or worrying that others may call us crazy for even suggesting there is such a thing as magic. We fail to realize that those limitations are imposed upon us by society, not the universe itself.

We are born believing in magic. Not because anyone told us to, but because we can clearly see the world through our own eyes. Adults often dismiss the "invisible friends" of children, yet there are plenty of family stories about children sharing messages and having conversations with deceased loved ones, even if the child never met the person when they were alive.

Think back to things you saw or did as a child that were shrugged off as play or a creative imagination. Maybe you were like me and talked to the plants, trees, and animals in the yard or around the block. You had a sense of every crevice and nook, maybe knew things about your home or neighborhood that no one else did. There were places that felt special and wonderful, and spots you stayed away from. You could hear the river speak in the morning and the ocean sing at night. Details that others overlooked stood out to you right away.

As you got older, you might have been teased about or otherwise dissuaded from discussing these experiences. They were "not natural" or "crazy"—as if connecting with nature or communing with your surroundings was somehow unnatural or not sane (rather the opposite!). But whatever the reason, you may have stopped seeing, speaking, or acknowledging that part of yourself. You became disconnected.

As adult magical practitioners, we spend so much time breaking down those walls we allowed society to construct around our mind. We long to be reconnected to those mysteries and re-enchant how we see the world. We actively seek to reengage and strengthen that psychic vision we had as children.

Even if some of what we experienced as children does fall under fantasy and playtime, that's not necessarily a bad thing either. Being able to play, explore ideas, and be creative are important life skills that are often severely underappreciated in modern society. We have the potential to create new realities, whether that's composing a piece of music, making a painting, designing spaces that are accessible to more people, or finding new ways to look at data to discover cures for diseases. In order to create, we need to be open to imagining what is possible, even if others deem it impossible. In fact, that's even more of a reason to try—to fly over those perceived blocks and limitations.

Magic starts with thought, and using your imagination is absolutely a gateway to magic. Being able to picture in some way what you wish to accomplish is at the heart of manifestation. If a song can get your body moving, a painting can move you to tears, a smart design can improve your quality of life, and research can save lives, then clearly thought has an impact on us. What started as an invisible essence in your mind can influence and change the world in very real, tangible ways. This knowledge is the first mystery revealed by the Witch Lungs.

Breathe Better

Now that you've started to get a sense of your metaphysical lungs, let's take a moment to check in with the physical ones. This will help in the next sections as we learn more about the Witch Lungs and explore practices we can utilize to engage them.

Without shifting your body or changing position, slowly breathe in through your nose, and pay attention to how the air feels as it enters your nasal cavity and passes through the back of your throat and down to your chest, expanding your lungs—then release it softly and feel it all rush out. Repeat this two more times, following the path of the air in and out, in and out.

Next adjust your posture so that you are sitting (or standing) more upright, lifting your sternum slightly and allowing your shoulders to roll back (if they were hunched forward). Breathe in deeply again and feel how much deeper into your chest the air gets. You probably were not even aware of how much your breathing was impacted by your relaxed posture.

Another technique you can do is to lightly place your hands loosely crossed over your heart area but not directly touching it. Allow about a kitten of space between your hands and your chest. As you breathe in, focus on your sternum. As your chest rises, gently separate your hands while also lifting your chin up. As you exhale, your body may relax, but keep your chin up and your hands in front of you. You'll still be properly upright for a good breathing position. You can also use the visualization of the sun rising out from your chest as you breathe in and the sun setting as you exhale.

Most of us go about our daily lives getting just the barest amount of air because of our posture. Whether you work at a desk in front of a computer or are on your feet, check in with your posture regularly. Setting an alarm with a reminder may help you get started on the road to being more aware of your posture and breath. Once you get the hang of it, you'll feel more awake, aware, and prepared—simply because you are breathing more efficiently!

Interconnectivity and the Spirit of Everything

If you were able to look inside your lungs, this view would reveal a structure that looks just like the branches of a tree. This resemblance is especially uncanny when you recall that trees create the very air we breathe. Trees are truly the lungs of the Earth, and our own body's structure reflects that. If we need reminding that we are intimately connected to the world, all we have to do is breathe.

With every inhalation, we bring the outside world within us. With every exhalation, we release a part of ourselves into the world. Everything around us is participating in this exchange in its own way—and not just the plants and animals. Think of the salty air by an ocean or of petrichor, the smell of earth after a rainfall. A newly forming volcano erupting and fungi feeding off of the decomposing forest floor both contribute to the atmosphere. We are all sharing molecules.

Embracing interconnectivity is vital, as we need to care about one another and the environment we live in. We are in a relationship with the universe— and every important relationship should be founded on respect. If as a society we were much more conscious of the pattern we are a part of, the overculture would be more firmly rooted in compassion, understanding, and communication. The message would be one of mutual respect for and acknowledgment of our resources, including the integral components of life, from the tiniest organisms to the planet itself.

As Witches, it's not enough to just acknowledge the living things we can easily identify with as humans; we need to expand our understanding beyond that as well. When we start to recognize these connections, we realize there is more to the world. We begin to perceive and interact with liminal realms and spirits.

For as long as I can remember, I have talked to everything: trees, insects, doors, birds, coats, the ocean, electronics, my paintbrushes, my room—basically everything animate and inanimate that I come into contact with. I think I had an innate sense from the beginning that we're all made up of the same particles, and if I had a consciousness, so must they. Throughout my journey as a Witch, this idea has only been supported and deepened by what I've experienced along the way. I didn't know there was a name for this concept until I began exploring other spiritual paths in my teens. Derived from the Latin word *anima*, meaning "breath, spirit, life," animism centers around the idea that everything, whether it be an object, a place, a plant, or an animal, has a distinct spiritual essence or conscious spark. Animism gives a greater sense of identity and presence to everything around us, seen and unseen, natural and human-made. The lines between the physical and spiritual worlds become blurred, if not altogether nonexistent. Distinctions of life and agency seen as belonging solely to human beings expand to include animals, plants, and places, as well as immaterial entities. Today I am rather excited to see animistic concepts introduced to the larger culture as a gentle means of guidance, improvement, and awareness for emotional, mental, physical, and spiritual well-being. Whether it shows up in a cartoon or a show about decluttering, I think that is a wonderful sign.

I feel it's also worthwhile to bring up two other similar concepts: hylozoism and panpsychism. Hylozoism is a philosophical theory that says all matter is in some sense alive, but it doesn't necessarily assign a consciousness to it as well. One way to put this idea into context is that our cells are alive, and also made up of smaller organelles—all of which are made up of atoms, which are also alive. But those atoms and cells being alive doesn't mean they are also conscious. Panpsychism, on the other hand, suggests that everything physical contains an individual consciousness that collectively contributes to reality. Panpsychism tends to delineate the level or state of active consciousness depending on the physical form. For example, rocks are "sleeping," wolves are "dreaming," and humans are "waking"—while the divine itself is fully awake.

The distinctions made by both hylozoism and panpsychism are invested in a hierarchy that elevates humans above everything else (except God). But the aspects we can take from their base ideas—that matter is energy that is alive, and that everything has an essence—factors well into magic and Witchcraft. Animism as a concept gives more agency, more conscious equality or equity, across the board to the divine spark, regardless of what form it presents as.

People do tend to unconsciously restrict themselves to the spirits of things they can communicate with. But even if we feel we are unable to communicate with something, that doesn't mean it lacks essence or spirit. That has more to do with our capabilities and limits of understanding than anything else. There are other ways of being and existing outside of the human experience. Nature doesn't have a motive; it simply is. We like to apply human reasoning to explain why other beings do what they do—be that a tree, a wolf, a virus, a bee, a fish, or a cow. We may connect weather patterns like hurricanes, tornadoes, and droughts with a moral incentive (or deterrent), but that comes down to blame versus blessing. Human activities certainly impact the planet, which we should be conscious of, but everything beyond that is about cause and effect within the pattern of life.

We and everything around us are made of star stuff. We recognize that different combinations of atoms and states of matter appear to mark where we end and the book, cat, or table begins. The point where animism can get mind-boggling is when we consider if everything is an individual spirit, or are we part of a collective consciousness? Do we have identity outside of that essence? If we see that the mountain has a spirit, then so does the boulder that crashes down from it, and the rock that broke off of it, and the gravel and sand worn away from it. I find it really interesting to think how animism can definitely start to change the way we see spirit being present in the world.

So go ahead and talk to things, take their measure and meaning in your life. Connect more deeply and consciously with the space around you and what exists within it. Consider the spaces in between and the spirits of places and things—as the wise Witch does.

◎ JOURNAL PROMPT ◎
Connecting with Spirit

- *Artifact:* Is there an object that is very special to you? If it's accessible to you, take a few moments to look it over physically, feel it, and consider where it came from, how it was made, and any people who may have been involved with the making or meaning of it. How did it come to you and when? Which of those physical factors especially influence how you feel or think about it? Does the object seem to have an energy of its own?

- *Place:* Is there a favorite place where you like to sit (indoors or outside)? What draws you to it? If you could assign a personality to that place, what would that be? What elements or features lead you to this association? Has it ever not felt that way to you, and why do you think that is?

- *Plant Being:* Is there a tree you see on a regular basis that you always notice? Maybe it's one that is close to where you live or that you notice when you go on a trip. The next time you see it, consider what your emotional response is to the tree. What basic information do you get just from looking at it? Look at how its branches and leaves are, the way its trunk is formed, what it is situated near, etc. What do you think the tree has seen in its time? Is there anyone or anything the tree reminds you of? Is there anything you could do for the tree?

✷ 3 Breaths Exercise ✷

Breath can be a powerful tool for focusing both your mind and your body. Whether I'm about to perform dance, lead a ritual, teach a workshop, or any other activity that may require significant focus, I take three slow, deep breaths. When I can, I do this exercise using the whole of my body to conduct the air in and out—meaning my arms and legs are involved in the process.

1. To start, stand with your legs a little wider than shoulder-width apart, with a bit of squishy bend in your knees, and have your arms loosely crossed in front of your diaphragm.

2. As you take a deep breath in, lower your center of gravity slightly by bending your knees while also uncrossing and extending your arms outward in a welcoming position.

3. Hold the breath for three seconds, then slowly release, bringing your arms back to center while slightly straightening your legs.

4. Repeat the whole movement again, this time holding your breath for six seconds and then releasing.

5. Lastly, follow the process one more time, holding for nine seconds and then releasing the breath.

You should feel calm, collected, and ready to accomplish the task at hand. Now, while using the whole body tends to give the best results, you can certainly modify this exercise to suit your needs, including being completely still, sitting, or even lying down if you need to. The 3 Breaths exercise is also a handy technique for helping you to relax your mind when you're getting ready for bed.

Sovereignty of the Witch

One of the most defiant and powerful things we can do as Witches is to claim our space, starting with our very own body. The Witch has a strong sense of self, independent and fully aware of their own power and agency. The Witch claims the right to personal governance while also acknowledging their responsibility.

Understanding that you are interconnected and part of nature—not separate from it—does not discount your sense of self. The concept of sovereignty focuses on the power of a body or being to govern itself, without interference from outside sources or other beings. While there will of course be outside influences—as is the nature of being part of the universal pattern—sovereignty is about acknowledging and honoring your sense of self regardless. Witchcraft is not about having power or authority over others, but rather over yourself.

In Modern Traditional Witchcraft, there are three main keys that all factor into this concept of sovereignty:

- Know thyself
- Maintain balance
- Accept responsibility

"Know thyself" seems like it should be an easy thing, but it's not. This concept is about being aware of not only all of your strengths and good traits but also your flaws and weaknesses—not for the purpose of inflating your ego or picking yourself apart, but rather of having a realistic map of yourself. If you focus only on the good or the bad, you will miss opportunities to challenge yourself and grow your wisdom.

In terms of sovereignty, "maintain balance" is applied in being conscious about what you give and what you take energetically. This key reminds you not only to take care of yourself, but also to take care of others. In terms of the Witch Lungs, you must find a rhythm of breath that works for you, lest you become overwhelmed or worn out.

As for "accept responsibility," I find that Heron Michelle summed it up beautifully in her Patheos blog, *Witch on Fire*: "We take responsibility for the world we create.... We also affirm our interdependence within the web of existence ... the matrix that weaves us together, the ground of being.[...]Yes, to be sovereign means *you are in charge of you.* You have authority over your own life, mind, heart, will, body and spirit."[2]

To add to that, if you choose to ignore your own warning signs or unbalance yourself repeatedly, that is also your responsibility. It's not about placing blame on someone else or yourself, but about becoming wise to the ways of probability, pattern, and consequence. With experience as a guide, you can learn to do better in the future.

What does sovereignty feel like in regard to being a Witch? Sovereignty is a sense of wholeness, of feeling centered in your body, yet this power is also flowing out around you like a fountain. There's a near-subconscious or subliminal sense of your own divine presence and connection with the world. That may sound egotistical, but again, sovereignty is not based in power over other things or people; it's authority over yourself. Once you have achieved this state, it's very much like breathing.

Breath is something we typically don't think about—it's an involuntary process. We're not consciously thinking about it—until we are—like when we might be out of breath from running, dealing with high elevations, or fighting off an asthma or allergy attack. Similarly, we tend not to think about our boundaries or authority until they're being infringed upon by someone or something else.

That often involuntary nature doesn't mean you can't learn to feel sovereign. Rather, it just takes a bit of practice and building body familiarity with the feeling of recognizing yourself as sovereign. For example, when I teach ritual movement and dance, I always start with posture—addressing how the body feels from toe to head rather than how you may appear in the mirror. (See the Aligning the Bodies exercise in chapter 4.) The posture may feel unfamiliar at first, but as you begin to work with it, your body adjusts and you start to do it naturally on a daily basis. Just as the invisible can affect the visible,

2. Heron Michelle, "The Paradox of Personal Sovereignty in Modern Witchcraft," *Witch on Fire* (blog), *Patheos*, March 19, 2018. https://www.patheos.com/blogs/witchonfire/2018/03/paradox-personal-sovereignty/.

the physical can certainly have a way of impacting your emotional and mental consciousness as well. Building a practice that helps you become familiar with the sensation of sovereignty starts with connecting the physical body with the mental, emotional, and spiritual.

✳ A Spell for Summoning the Sovereign Self ✳

No external supplies or tools are required for this spell, but you can augment it by lighting a white candle before starting. You can also perform it while facing a mirror if you'd like to amplify the effect. This is a good working to do in the morning as you get ready for the day, or at night before you go to bed.

Take a deep breath in, focusing on the air entering your chest, and visualize vibrant light or energy particles filling you. Then slowly exhale, again visualizing what that air might look like if you could see it leave your body and join with the world. Repeat this again two more times, and with each breath, visualize that energy going beyond your lungs into the rest of your body.

Say:

> *My breath is my being, my being is my breath.*
> *My body and spirit are my own, even through death.*
> *Being Witch embodied, my power is my own*
> *I know this to be true in my blood, breath, and bone.*

Breath Gives Rise to Voice

Your ability to speak is rooted in the functions of the respiratory system. Whether you are singing, screaming, whispering, or speaking, all of these are powered by manipulation of your breath. With intent and focus, the voice can be used to soothe, heal, warn, incite, inspire, command, or charm. Your voice is one of your most powerful means of communication, regardless of whether what you say is spoken or written.

The voice is a conduit for magic, and so much potential opens up when you recognize that fact. Think about it: the words you say are heard by someone else—and that idea has now been transferred from your mind to theirs. You can make someone picture something, understand a situation, or feel an emotion simply by speech or song. Through the power of air and breath, the invisible is transmitted and takes form.

It can be all too easy to overlook the power your voice has, to take your own words for granted. You might be too loose with your words, stripping them of meaning, or you might let others speak for you, erasing your presence when you should be counted. There is a balance between knowing when to speak and when to be silent. Alas, you might figure out what that line is only once you've passed it. I'm sure you can easily recall a time when you said too much or didn't speak up when you should have. There's nothing good that comes out of beating yourself up about a mistake in the past. Instead, you can try to use that experience to do better.

You can train yourself to be more mindful of your words when you do choose to speak. Then you won't be wasting your breath with unnecessary words. You can also use your voice wisely to make a greater impact when the time comes to be heard.

⊚ JOURNAL PROMPT ⊚
Power of Words

Words have power, largely through our associations with them. What word or phrase do you find

- the most beautiful?
- energizing or exhilarating?
- anxiety- or dread-inducing?
- the most calm or relaxing?
- the most powerful or strong?

What makes you feel that way about each word or phrase? Is there an experience linked to that word? Is there a word or phrase that feels especially magical to you? Why?

Wise Word Sigil

In today's society, people have a tendency to rush about, not taking the time to fully comprehend what they're being presented with, while also feeling like they must respond immediately. Ill-prepared responses often create a cacophonous feedback loop, raising stress levels and causing additional conflict. This sigil helps reduce miscommunication while fostering critical thinking, comprehension, and active listening. A little magic to help us with communication can go a long way.

The Wise Word Sigil has the following built into it:

- Focuses attention on the heart of the matter and the intent of the message/word
- Enhances the ability to understand what's being communicated
- Encourages new and creative thought patterns to increase comprehension
- Promotes balanced listening and learning, quieting the noise
- Interrupts feedback loops of a negative nature while aiding positive interaction
- Prevents knee-jerk, uninformed, disrespectful, and/or irrelevant responses
- Instills contemplation and deeper thinking

This sigil is best placed at centers of communication: on computers or phones or in meeting places. It can be used for meditation or carved into a candle, which can be lit during discussion times. It's also handy to use when reciting or delivering a speech, drafting communication, writing prose/poems, or making an important phone call.

Wise Word Sigil

Creating and Being Magical Space

There are two kinds of magical spaces to be addressed in this section: our bodies and the working space surrounding them, often known as the magic circle or sacred sphere. As the Witch Lungs occupy the space within and without (what we breath/take in, what we breath/give out), this is a wonderful way to connect with them.

If Witches view the world as sacred, then why do we need to create specifically defined magical space? It's easy to get caught up in semantics, rules, and traditions, but there are many good reasons why we create special space to work in, which we're about to explore.

First, it's important to understand that many of us live in a culture that has long been hinged on the opposing binary categories of sacred versus profane, or, to a lesser extent, the separation of the sacred and the secular. Because of this imposed delineation, we have a tendency to want to designate space in those terms automatically. Since we have been taught to think that way, that separation naturally affects our view on magical spaces. But when we start to consider the histories that have enforced this divide, toxicity can be revealed. The doctrines that say that "God is only present in *these* places or with *those* people" have negatively influenced society for far too long. So many wars have been fought over segregated divinity and a religiously divined right to certain places, peoples, and positions of power. When we see the world as sacred, we reject the binary construct that seeks to divide people and places from the divine. We shift how we see and experience magical space.

That's not to say we can't have certain places that are extra special to us. We need only look around the planet at temples and churches that have been the center of some sacred activity in one form or another for thousands of years, through a multitude of religions and practices. Places that are home to devotional rituals and practice definitely take on a different sort of resonance, even centuries after the last devotee made their offerings there. Another way to look at temples and churches is that they are dedicated spiritual workspaces. Often their main purpose is as a place of community gathering, but they can also be the earthly residence of a specific deity or spirit. These locations may also serve as a school, a residence for clergy, or a place of spiritual commerce and services such as divination, healing, or the bestowing of sacraments.

Religious persecution, enforced diaspora, environmental destruction, land theft—all of these things have played a role in the loss of designated sacred space for many Witches and magical practitioners. So while we Witches have our favorite spots, we have long developed the ability to be mobile with our practices. Not being tied down to one location can lead us to flex our magical muscles and help us to recognize that we carry sacred space with us.

Another way to think about magical space is that it is primarily designated working space. An altar (as we learned with the Magician) is a place of action. Ideally the environment should be conducive to helping you successfully do whatever activity you have in mind. The process of cleaning, preparing, and delineating space is done in order to get the best results. Just as I prefer to sit down at a clean desk with good lighting and all of my tools within easy reach when I want to create, the same is true for a magic circle.

Circles, spheres, and other magical shapes are crafted to collect energy, to contain or protect, to separate, to be a communing space or meeting ground, to craft a liminal space between worlds, or to orient oneself with specific spirits of place, elements, or deities. A magical space may act as a virtual temple or a protected doorway to opening communication across realms. A common phrase you will hear about a circle is that it is a place that is not a place, in a time that is not a time.

A lot of books on magic and Witchcraft include very precise parameters about how big a circle should be, what tools you need, the words you must say to make the circle, and how to deconstruct it. Much of that information is often rooted in modern Western occultism—which is to say methods inspired by ceremonial magic and grimoire traditions. They are *a* way to create magic space, but definitely not the only way or necessarily the best way, depending on your needs and your path.

Your space can be as large or as small as you need it, from encircling your home to being just outside of your physical body. You can acknowledge directions and call in elements, spirits, and deities—or not. You don't need a single tool other than your body to make the circle or sphere.

That said, I think knowing a bit about the why things may be done a certain way can be helpful. Many magic circles are cast by calling in the element of Air from the east to begin and the element of Earth in the north to finish. Why those two specific directions? With circles starting in the east, the association is often with the rising of the sun. With this symbolism, when the circle is fully cast, you have referenced the whole cycle of day and night—yet you are also working outside of time and place. The north is considered to be a place of darkness, death, spirits, and mystery, so ending in the north recognizes the journey of life—out of darkness we were born, and to darkness we return. In the space between Earth and Air, north and east, we tap into that liminal space between life and death, remembering that we begin and end with breath.

Other methods of casting a circle involve working with the concept of a compass or crossroads. Often in these cases, the space is worked not only in a circular motion but also back and forth across the space, forming an X or +, which makes the center a focal point. It's much like the junction of an X-axis and a Y-axis on a graph, which is called the origin in mathematics. In that sense, we are marking the coordinates of where we are, orienting ourselves in time and space. We are claiming our space and making our presence known in all directions: north and south, east and west, above and below, within and without.

Is one way more correct or effective? Well, it largely comes down to symbolism and practice. All elements exist in all places, so the attribution of them to certain directions is an example of humans applying order to the natural state of things. We are again using symbol as a touchstone for understanding larger mysteries. It's also much easier to do a group working if everyone involved understands that we associate this element with this direction and this color, per the rulebooks. But which colors, elements, and directions are aligned will vary from practice to practice, tradition to tradition, region to region. Regardless, these correlations and methods all must work for someone if they continue to be used. The symbolism points to something real, no matter how you spin it. What matters most is finding meaning in what you're doing, which means you will know why you're doing it that way.

When creating magical space, consider your needs and what it is you wish to accomplish.[3] That will help you determine what will work best for you. The more you practice your path, the more you will understand that a "one size fits all" approach is not helpful when considering or creating magical space. There is definitely power in having a traditional or prescribed method, as it taps into one kind of established pattern. But there is need and room for a lot more fluidity in Modern Traditional Witchcraft. Not every circle needs to be an air-sealed container, especially if you wish to work with land spirits and foster other kinds of connections. Think of crafting magical space like wearing a scuba suit (self-contained underwater breathing apparatus): If you're going to be diving deep underwater, it's a great tool. On land, the same suit will weigh you down and restrict what you can do. If you just want to snorkel on the surface of the water, all you need is a proper lightweight mask and maybe some fins. Select the method and approach that correlates with the task at hand.

Now that we have an understanding of what magical space is in terms of creating working space, let's focus on the one you are in right this moment that doesn't take any planning: your body. Your body is your primary tool for casting external sacred space, but it is also the origin of your physical and metaphysical selves. The practice we're about to explore can be done anywhere, whenever you need it, for countless reasons. It's also an excellent primer for expanding the presence of your body. We will build on this method for creating external magical space later in chapter 7, once we've become fully familiar with the anatomy of the Witch.

✳ The Circle of the Body ✳

While your body may not technically be circle-shaped, it runs on cycles within a relatively contained space: breath going in and out, blood cycling through the heart, nerves sending signals back and forth down the spine. Your body is also the culmination of all of the elements combined: Air as breath; Water as blood and other fluids; Fire as internal combustion through your heart beating, digestion,

---

3. We will delve deeper into ritual and the reasons for crafting it in the next chapter, so don't worry if you're not yet sure how to make those determinations. We are discussing circle-casting and magical space here mainly because it is an aspect of the Witch Lungs.

as well as electric nerve pulses; Earth as your skin and bones; and Spirit as the essence of your mind. Body and Spirit intersect to make up a crossroads meeting of you. Everything that some folks say you need to call into a circle is already present in your body.

To consciously focus on your body as magical space, do the 3 Breaths exercise to prepare. Close your eyes. Breathe in, and as the air hits your nasal cavity and heads down into your chest, think, "(I am) Air and Fire." Then as you exhale, focus on sending the air down to your belly and your feet, thinking, "(I am) Water and Earth." You could also simply visualize colors (yellow, red, blue, green). Breathe in visualizing red and yellow, and exhale with green and blue. Just that one breath in and out does the trick. You have acknowledged the elements within your own body and can start to do whatever work you need. If that seems a little too fast for you, start off by focusing on one element/color per breath in and out. As your brain and body get the hang of it, you will be able to do all of the elements with one whole breath cycle.

◐ WITCHUAL ◑
Circle of Air

Consider casting a circle just to focus on the element of Air—no other elements involved. The nature of such a circle could focus on germinating thought and inspiration and sparking new beginnings. Dispel the circle using the same technique, focusing on completion, endings, and releasing.

✳ Targeted Breath ✳

Slow breaths can calm you down, while quicker inhalations speed up your heart rate. You tend to learn to connect the speed of your breath with your overall state as a child (usually in gym class). But have you ever given thought to the direction of your breath? Thanks to the design of our bodies, you can combine breath with intention to awaken or energize certain areas. Your respiratory tract begins at your nostrils, so when you breathe in, that air travels up into your nasal cavity, then down your trachea into the bronchial tubes, filling your lungs as the diaphragm contracts to expand your chest.

This path touches upon three vital areas: the head, the heart, and the belly. Each of these zones can benefit from targeted breath. By that I mean focusing your attention on that specific area as you inhale. So if I were to say, "Breathe into your head," you become more conscious of the air as it travels into your nasal cavity and down your throat. When you "breathe into your heart," your attention centers on the air as it passes into the bronchial tubes, close to where your heart is situated. Lastly, when you "breathe in your belly," you become more acutely aware of the movement of your diaphragm, which is adjacent to your abdominal cavity. Technically, where your breath goes anatomically doesn't change. However, the directional mental alignment of the breath can certainly have an impact on the area you are focusing on.

- To seek mental clarity and connect with others, breathe into your head.
- To gain emotional balance and focus on the task at hand, breathe into your heart.
- To foster healing and promote physical well-being, breathe into your belly.

Aroma and the Magic of Smells

Air is an element of communication. We talked about the power of voice and words earlier, but there are forms of communicating associated with the element of Air that we can explore through the Witch Lungs.

The sense of smell is one of the oldest and most primal. Even if you cannot see or are hard of hearing (and as long as you're not stuffed up with a cold), your nose can help guide the way to safety as well as warn you. Your nose can guide you toward food, water, and places that are safe, as well as potential partners. The nose can also alert you to dangerous situations, such as when food or drink is unfit for consumption, if possible predators are nearby, as well as sickness and disease in people, animals, or places.

Air and aroma play a major role in nature, the propagation of life, and magic. Flowers have scents that attract pollinators, and pollen itself can be spread on breezes. Tiny particles are being exchanged to create new life by those on wing and by the winds. The aroma of a flower or the parts of an herb can help you connect with that plant spirit as well. Many kinds of animals make use of scent through musk (glandular secretions) to attract mates or mark their territory. Humans have long turned to the aromas of both plants and animals to draw power in some way—by making themselves smell more attractive, by sharing scents to express sentiments of romance or some other intent, or to take on symbolic properties of plant or animal using sympathetic magic.

Smoke and incense also function on the level of aroma as communication. All around the world, you will find the use of smoke cleansing. Basically this process involves burning dried herbs, wood, resins, and other safely burnable materials in order to metaphysically cleanse or purify a space, being, or object. Sage, mugwort, cedar, and juniper are just a few herbs that are used in cleansing and purification rituals because they are believed to drive away unwanted entities and energies. While smoke cleansing tends to focus on clearing out, the burning of incense is used for the opposite effect: to draw something in or add to a space, being, or object. Special blends of incense are used to attract or feed spirits, honor ancestors, please or appease deities, bless objects, and transform spaces. The smoke of particular incenses and burnable offerings is used to send messages, either on this plane or to other realms and beings.

Aroma is also deeply intertwined with memory. When I smell bell peppers being roasted, I am instantly transported back to my grandparents' home in South Philadelphia. The scent of a certain perfume or cologne can bring back vivid memories of a favorite lover. The smell of a person you no longer care for can become repulsive to you, even if you were friends with them originally. Think about an aroma that transports you every time you smell it. You might even find yourself noticing scent as a metaphysical message from a loved one who has passed on, with there being no other way to account for a particular smell. There is magic to be tapped into with your sense of smell.

You can alter a situation by introducing scents that have emotional or physiological effects (as long as you don't have allergies or scent-related migraines). For example, in terms of aromatherapy, lavender generally calms and relaxes people, while rosemary stimulates (and also has the magical association of aiding memory). Burning frankincense is said to help fight depression. Incense, candles, and other aromatic mixes can help create an atmospheric background for your ritual workings, setting the mood and attracting what you desire into the space. Anointing the body with selected scented oils can help set the mood either for a day or for a specific ritual. I have an array of oils that I apply to the insides of my wrists after my morning bath. I don't heavily douse myself, as I'm aware of other people's sensitivities, but it's just enough for me to smell in the morning as it mixes with my own body chemistry.

To start accessing your nasal wisdom more effectively, begin by taking a moment to consciously sample the air. When you go outside, what does the air smell like? Can you tell anything about the weather or what's happening in the ecosystem around you? What's blooming or decomposing? When you enter a building or arrive in a new city, take in the smells and process your immediate emotional or mental responses to them. When you meet someone new, how does their scent make you feel? When working in the garden, take time to smell what you're working with, whether it's the soil or things you are putting in or weeding out. When you're cooking, smell the ingredients and note how they may change throughout the cooking process. These little details can communicate a lot of information.

◎ JOURNAL PROMPT ◎
Sensing Scent

Consciously considering what associations certain smells have for you can be very useful in applying them in ritual and spellcraft. Consider what aromas are pleasing or repugnant to you, and see if you can determine why you feel that way about that smell.

- What scent is calming or soothing for you?
- What scent invigorates you or makes you feel powerful?
- What scent do you associate with cleaning, cleansing, and purification?
- Is there a certain incense or scent that you associate with a spirit, deity, or ancestor that you might work with?

Considering Pollution

Pollution is the introduction of something harmful into an environment that can cause damage or destruction. The danger of becoming attuned with the world is that sometimes you run the risk of becoming too permeable or susceptible to certain kinds of pollution. There are no immediate barriers between the air you breathe and your lungs, though you can certainly apply filters and masks. With your Witch Lungs, you must take precautions against being too open or functioning without filters.

You can view pollution as physical or metaphysical, with each sometimes manifesting similar effects. This can include people seeking to invade your space, or your own unhealthy habits that are damaging to your mental or physical health. Suspect information, intentions, and influences that seek to harm can all fall under pollution. But to totally shut out the world or be oblivious to it is playing it safe or being willfully ignorant. Ignoring spirit and other connections out of fear can cause even more harm or create bigger obstacles.

Witches cannot block out absolutely everything and successfully do their work. We have to allow room for growth. So we must remember to protect ourselves accordingly. We can have boundaries, protect our space effectively, and practice upholding our sovereignty. As we move further into the Witch's anatomy, we'll find more ways to both protect and empower ourselves.

✳ A Charm to Ward Against Pollution ✳

With breath of air so fresh, I summon the winds of change
To banish that which is harmful far out of my range!

Witch Lungs Sigil

Sigils are human-made symbols infused with magical properties. They can be used for many things including simplified spells, devotional gateways, focal points, wards, and markers. The ones you will find in this book at the end of each chapter have been especially created to aid you on your journey through the anatomy of the Witch.

Use the Witch Lungs Sigil as a meditational focus for strengthening your Witch Lungs. You could carve it on a candle, draw it for your altar, or anoint it on your chest. Begin with the 3 Breaths exercise, recite the poem at the beginning of this chapter, then apply the sigil in the method you have chosen. Revisit this sigil whenever you need to focus on the lessons of the Witch Lungs.

Witch Lungs Sigil

Chapter 2
Witch Heart

The Heart sees what the mind cannot know,
Hung in our chests, a drum to the flow.
Blood pulsing in, pattern weaving out,
Marking the tides of ritual route.
Every drop was once part of a star,
Still today reminds us who we are.

Rooted in the chest, the heart sits nestled between the lungs. Veins and arteries branch out throughout the body, intricate highways bringing blood to and fro. Every tiny capillary, vein, and artery connects back to the heart, mapping a network through the body. The heart is situated at the crossroads of all of these circulatory roads, drumming out the pulse of life one beat at a time. When it stops, we also come to a halt. Essentially, the heart is what moves us. Hence, as we breathe, we beat and pulse, flaming the spark of life.

The Witch Heart sets the pulse for practice, awakening our emotions with its beats, granting us vision, and moving us forward on our paths. Witches tap into universal rhythms, following the beat of their heart to find their way. Wisdom flows within our veins, the capacity for knowledge ever expanding.

Blood takes the information and essence that the Witch Lungs bring in and disseminates them to the body through the Witch Heart—to feed the spirit, to remove what is not needed or harmful, and to refresh and renew us. These are the benefits that ritual provides us with. Ritual takes the spiritual and invisible essence and encapsulates it in such a way to bring meaning and potency to the pattern of our lives. It helps make us who we are, defining our path and process. In turn, the ritual becomes us and we become the ritual.

The Priestess
Walk the mystery.

The Magician has prepared the way for the Priestess by setting up the altar, positioning the tools, and preparing the space to be worked in. Now is the time to figure out how things work, what these tools mean to you, and how to implement them effectively. Part of this process sometimes involves learning things the hard way, as in what not to do in comparison to what works best. In order to figure out this practice, you have to do more than just stand there. You need to have a plan, which means you will need to gather information to plot accordingly. Hence the mode of the Priestess is to help build expertise through experimentation and experience. Moving forward can be scary, but all you need to do is take a breath and jump in.

Within the realm of the Priestess is the mystery of things hidden in the depths of consciousness, the subtle influences of the world around you as well as inner illumination. Associated with the number 2, this card comes with a sense of duality and communication. When you gaze upon the Priestess, you may note the lunar phases in her crown, the solar cross on her chest, and the crescent at her feet. She is flanked by black and white temple pillars. Within these symbols you can find a balance of light and shadow, night and day—touching upon the lunar and solar cycles of ritual. Through ritual, not only is a motif established but also the pattern is revealed.

The Priestess beckons you to enter the mystery: not just to look the part, but to walk the path, even if you're unsure of where it leads. Not everything can be neatly planned out or predicted. You have to turn your eyes away from the map to see where you are going. Within you, you carry a flame to light your way and a drum to set the pace. You must listen to the rhythm within to figure out what works best for you, as what works for someone else may not be the best practice for you. Start with a simple beat, light the candle, and let ritual flow out from there.

I Like to Move It, Move It

The heart is a muscle that makes motion possible by pumping blood through our bodies. The Witch Heart helps us apply meaning and purpose to that movement. Its rhythm helps us focus on what's important to our path and practice.

"The Cauldron of Poesy," a medieval Irish bardic poem,[4] describes three spiritual cauldrons found within the human body, located in the head, chest, and belly regions. Aptly named, the Cauldron of Motion is located approximately where our heart and lungs are situated. This cauldron emphasizes the idea that what moves us, makes us. As in, what makes our pulse quicken with excitement and stirs our soul into action defines us.

Similarly, in the numerous spiritual theories that propose a three-part spirit, the heart is where the Talking or Conscious Self is said to reside. This self is concerned with our cognitive and emotional well-being. We think of the heart as the core of our emotional selves. The heart is a place of consideration—we may talk about how something may weigh heavy upon our heart as we seek balance. When we speak of getting to the heart of the matter, we're describing the most essential part of a situation, the crux of something important.

The heartbeat is comfort. As you grew in the womb, you heard the beating of your parent's heart and the pulsing of blood all around you. The sound is soothing and was the first beat you danced to as you took on physical form.

When was the last time you felt your own heartbeat or listened to the rhythm of a loved one's? The dance of life is happening one beat at a time within you, and in everyone around you. It's easy to get overwhelmed or distracted by all of the noise demanding your attention—or to strive for the more complex rhythm while overlooking the simple and steady one within your reach. Remember to check in with the beat of your own heart from time to time to center and guide you.

As Witches, while we may dance to the beat of our own drum, we're not looking to create discord. Nor do we seek dominion or power over the world. We strive for connection, unity, and balance with ourselves and the world

---

4. We will look at these cauldrons more closely in chapter 8.

around us. If we can allow ourselves to succumb to the rhythm, we flow into the universal pattern. Ritual helps us make room to be able to listen and connect more fully. Ritual should not separate us from the heartbeat or subvert it like a too-loud bass speaker at a concert. When we lose rhythm, we lose sight of path and purpose. When everything is seen as sacred and interconnected, small tasks and actions are just as powerful and effective as the big, lavish ones.

Another way to think about movement and the Witch Heart is through the expression "to light a fire under one's butt." The intent is to get someone to move physically or mentally. Fire is the element most strongly associated with the Witch Heart. (While Water may seem a more obvious choice because of blood, remember that all elements are present, each playing a part.) Ignited by air brought in by the Witch Lungs, the Witch Heart stokes the fire of our internal engine. That fire fuels our passion and gets us moving in all the right ways. When we move, we move the world.

With all this in mind, let us find out what it means to have a Witch's Heart and see where the crossroads can take us. There are many roads indeed to discover that all begin here. Calling to the blood that flows in our veins for guidance, it's time to set the pulse for our journey. Let's move it!

◎ JOURNAL PROMPT ◎
What Lights My Fire?

Consider what moves you—what is that *it* that ignites your inner passion? Is there something that really gets you excited, even if it may be difficult to achieve?

Far too often, we take on other people's expectations of us, and prioritize them ahead of what our needs are. I'm not talking about supporting friends and family or nurturing children, which often involves making sacrifices or accommodations for everyone to thrive. But rather I mean those times when we curtail our passion in order to be accepted or to avoid confrontation. Or when someone may have used their authority/position to get what they want or expect, versus taking our thoughts, feelings, goals, or even rights into consideration. During those times, we may hide or suppress that passion to just get by. Push all of that aside, and think about the flame you should be tending to.

Symbolism of the Heart

There is a wide variety of symbolism throughout the world that speaks to the power of the heart. Themes of identity, consciousness, and emotion show up and repeat throughout human history. The following is just a sampling of the symbols that speak of the magic of the heart.

In ancient Egyptian mythology, the heart was believed to be the seat or dwelling place of the soul. One of the most iconic images in Egyptian art is the scene of the "weighing of the heart." Found in many tombs, we get a vision of the Underworld where the jackal-headed god Anubis places the deceased's heart on a scale. On the other side of the scale is a feather, representing Ma'at, goddess of justice, truth, and universal order. If the heart didn't balance with the feather, the soul was eaten by the demon Ammit, the devourer of souls who was part lion, hippopotamus, and crocodile.

In Christian mythology, we find the Sacred Heart, which is a flaming heart with a crown of thorns, and often pierced by a sword or cross. It is associated with Jesus and the mysteries of the Virgin Mary, symbolizing the power of love and faith triumphing over sorrow and suffering. Both gruesome and powerful, the Sacred Heart likely influenced many of our more modern and secular visions of the heart. Without the religious trappings, the heart shape is most commonly associated with love, affection, and romance. The heart with an arrow through it harkens to Cupid's arrow finding its target, while a heart split into pieces represents heartache. When Valentine's Day rolls around, hearts appear aplenty, combined with chocolates, flowers, and shiny things.

In the minor arcana of the tarot, the suit of cups represents emotions, which is also aligned with the suit of hearts in a regular playing deck. We also see the heart featured prominently in the Three of Swords, as it is pierced on this card. The heart is essentially a cup or vessel for emotion, desire, and romance depicted throughout the tarot.

There are also expressions that relate the human heart with animal hearts, such as the heart of a lion (fierce and strong), the heart of a lamb or dove (gentle and kind), or the heart of a rabbit (fast and passionate). These idioms remind us that we closely associate the essence of a creature as being centralized in their heart. It is important to keep in mind that deep symbolism is involved here—working with animal energy does not require the actual heart of an animal.

Magic in Our Blood

Blood is the river of life and is considered by many to be a powerful tool for spellcraft and magic. Even just a little bit of blood can go a long way.

We associate blood with identity, sacrifice, connection, oaths, and power. In some magical traditions, initiations can involve blood being recorded in a book or shared to symbolize family connection. A drop of blood in certain spells and rituals may be used to make a devotional sacrifice or to create a sacred bond with another living being or spirit.

Often not talked about in magic circles, menstrual blood is believed to have great power. This blood can shed without sickness, injury, or death on a regular basis, hence the dodgy term "wound without healing." As it originates from the lining of the womb, menstrual blood can be associated with life-giving properties and sexual energy. It is not surprising that there are quite a few love spells that include menstrual blood as an ingredient. When you consider these things, the enormous number of taboos against menstruating make sense, concocted by those who feared it might be used against them.

There are also those who talk of "witch blood" as a way to describe the magical currents that run through our veins—either in a symbolic way or believed to be present in the blood physically. The latter in most cases tends to refer to family lineage, but that position can obviously go down a slippery slope tying genetics with magic in ways that are exclusionary and problematic.

Magic does indeed flow in our veins, but you certainly do not have to have a special pedigree or initiatory paperwork to prove it. The fact that you are here on this journey, sorting out the mysteries of the Magician, is all the proof required. Release superficial concepts of worth that may be imposed upon you by others. Devote your energy instead to understanding the cycles that blood can teach you about the wonder of yourself and the world around you. Blood travels through the crossroads of the heart and flows through the whole of your body. It knows your inner mysteries and workings better than anything else. Listen to the rituals it whispers with every heartbeat.

NOTE: Physically and metaphysically, blood is to be respected, regardless of where in the body it originates. While blood can be a powerful aid in working magic, it's important to keep in mind the hazards of bloodborne pathogens and illness. Any deliberate cuts made to draw blood should be done with a sterilized tool and proper dressing applied to the wound to prevent infection. Also, while menstrual blood doesn't require making a wound, there are still communicable diseases to consider. Subjecting others to your bodily fluids without consent is dangerous, irresponsible, and in many places illegal. Witch wisely, folks.

Bloodstream: Entering the Ritual

Take a moment to consider the physical composition of the blood running through your veins. Plasma (the liquid part) is made up largely of water, salts, and proteins—reminiscent of the primordial ocean from which life emerged on this planet. Plasma is essential for moving the solid particles of your blood for distribution throughout your body. Those solid particles are red blood cells, white blood cells, and platelets. Red blood cells are the oxygen delivery service, while white blood cells fight infection. Platelets aid with clotting when you have been injured.

The circulatory system makes a great metaphor for ritual. Our heart beats like a steady drum, providing a rhythm for life, while blood speaks to the connections that flow and keeps us moving. Blood follows a pattern created by our network of arteries, veins, and capillaries; it is pumped out to the very ends of the body and then returns again. The red blood cells refresh the rest of our body with oxygen and carry away what is no longer needed. Ritual can do the same for us: creating a rhythm for us to follow, invigorating our practice with a sense of meaning and purpose, and aiding us in removing and banishing what is unwanted in our lives. White blood cells protect us from infection and help us build immunity, and once again we find a parallel in ritual. We often perform rites when we need protection, blessings, and guidance. Much like platelets, we look to ritual to help us heal, to preserve our way of life, and to maintain or slow the flow when needed.

Before we go further, it's important to understand what ritual is and why it is so powerful. The Cambridge Dictionary defines ritual as "a set of fixed actions and sometimes words performed regularly, especially as part of a ceremony." But that definition barely scratches the surface and is likely part of the reason why so many people have a limited idea of ritual. Victor Turner, a British cultural anthropologist best known for his work on symbols, rituals, and rites of passage, described ritual as "a fusion of the powers believed to be inherent in the persons, objects, relationships, events, and histories which are represented by the ceremony itself."[5]

That definition does give us a better sense of what ritual is, but we might get hung up on associations we have with the word *ceremony*. Ritual does not have to be formal, grand, organized, or religious in nature. It can be, but for Witches especially, ritual is often far more organic, everyday, and practical. Essentially, ritual is done to bring meaning, purpose, and/or order to something. We are ritualistic beings and we do certain things every single day to create order in our lives and to get a sense of progress.

Human beings rely on both formal and informal ritual to set the pace for our lives. Just like how blood streams through both major arteries and tiny capillaries, there are many sizes and kinds of ritual to keep your practice active and flowing. Daily rituals help us engage with the everyday and feel connected. For special occasions, creating dynamic and elaborate ritual can provide powerful accents to our lives. Both have their place in the pattern.

Terry Pratchett, while predominantly a fiction writer, nonetheless nailed many aspects of magic and Witchcraft perfectly in his books. In *Pyramids*, the seventh book in his Discworld series, he writes: "Ritual and ceremony in their due times kept the world under the sky and the stars in their courses. It was astonishing what ritual and ceremony could do."[6] Pratchett is being playful here about the human tendency to overstress the effect of our ritual on the world around us. That somehow, if we miss doing a ritual on an exact date or

---

5. Victor W. Turner, "Symbols in African Ritual," *Science* 179, no. 4078 (March 16, 1973): 1102. http://www.jstor.org/stable/1734971.

6. Terry Pratchett, *Pyramids: The Book of Going Forth*, a Discworld novel (London: Corgi Books, 1990), 71.

time or don't perform a rite in a certain way, the world may be catastrophically affected. The world will likely go on with or without us and our rituals. In truth, we perform ceremonies for our own needs. We engage in ritual not only for ourselves, but also to feel connected to the mysteries and influential energies present in the universe. Ritual emphasizes our presence and participation in community and creation. We transcend our physical limitations to tap into something larger than ourselves. This relationship gives us a sense of agency—that we are playing an active or driving role in our own destiny.

There are just as many reasons for doing ritual as there are ways to do it. The primary thing regardless is to try and understand *why* you are doing it. Ritual done for ritual's sake can lose meaning and effect if you don't know why you keep it up or why you did it in the first place. The meaning does not have to be deep and spiritual. Sometimes we also discover deeper meaning and purpose in the repetition of an act, even if we didn't intend for that to happen when we started. We might try something new in order to solve a problem, find out it works for us, and desire to continue that practice. At the heart of ritual is crafting a pattern, regardless of whether it may seem minor or something that has a lot of pomp and circumstance. Some people think the more complex a ritual is, the better it will be. But more isn't necessarily better when it comes to ritual. Complexity isn't the factor that makes a ritual work—it's the understanding of what's involved and how it's done. It's okay to keep things simple.

Ritual is protocol encountering experience. If you can build ritual from a place of meaning, first and foremost, it starts to develop layers. Consider the following daily ritual: You brush your teeth in the morning and night because you know it's good hygiene, but over time it becomes something integral to how you craft your day. It makes you feel awake, clean, and ready to interact with the world. At night, dental care feels like tidying up and putting things in order. The same task can have different feelings and meanings just by the time of day and the order that you do it in.

Once you start to think about your daily activities, you will begin to uncover the layers of ritual and magic already present in your life. Later on in this chapter, you will explore how to expand on those everyday practices and craft effective ritual for more specific moments as well.

◎ JOURNAL PROMPT ◎
Magic in the Mundane

List five tasks or activities you do every day or every week that create order in your day-to-day life. What physical importance do they have in your life? What happens if you don't do them or get thrown off your schedule?

Now step outside of those physical effects and consider how you can view them from a more metaphysical perspective, or add a layer of magical meaning. Can that morning beverage help you set an intention for your day? Can a bath be used for spiritual cleansing or protection? What about meals?

The Tides of the Body

Anytime I am discussing ritual, magic, and the effects of the moon, I remind folks that we ourselves are largely bodies of water. For just as the moon affects the ocean tides with its phases, so too do we wax and wane, ebb and flow. We are essentially mobile oceans, and we too have tides.

This exercise is designed to help you connect with the flow of blood throughout your body. Not only will it help you become more in touch with the currents of your body, but it can also be a wonderful calming exercise.

Begin with the 3 Breaths exercise (in chapter 1) to prepare.

Place your right hand over your heart. Breathe in, centering the breath in your chest, filling your lungs. As you exhale, imagine the air as energy moving out from your lungs into your heart. Through your hand, feel the vibration of your heart beating as your chest gently collapses with the exhalation. From there (breathing normally), in your mind's eye, follow the flow of blood as it travels away from your heart. Section by section, you will follow the blood as it expands out through your body.

I recommend doing this exercise as slowly as possible to begin with. Counting each progression can be helpful, such as like this:

1. One…Your blood flows out of the heart and past the lungs like a gentle wave.

2. Two…Your blood travels north, reaching upward to your shoulders and neck.

3. Three…Your blood continues up your neck, reaching the brain, your eyes, your ears, your tongue, your nose.

4. Four…Your blood also works its way out of your shoulders, down your upper arms, and into your lower arms, wrists, palms, and fingers.

5. Five…Your blood also travels south through your torso and down to the hips, nourishing the liver, stomach, intestines, and kidneys as it goes.

6. Six…Your blood continues down your thighs, meeting your knees and going down into the calves and ankles and through the feet, all the way to your toes.

Your blood has fully reached all of your body. Remove your right hand from over your heart, and replace it with your left and take a deep breath. With this breath, call back the blood to your heart.

From here, reverse the count, starting at six with your toes and pulling the blood back like a wave gently receding—until you have reached the heart with the count of one. If you are feeling particularly out of sorts, you can really slow down the wave in both directions, across subsections of the body at each count instead of whole sections.

This process may also help you notice when something's off and needs attention, from physical discomforts to emotional blockages. If you come across something like this, spend extra time in that area, breathing blood into that area, breaking down the malcontent, and ebbing it away.

Over time, this exercise can also be speeded up so that the flow out is done in a single exhalation, and you inhale the blood back to center. The benefit of this very brief version (after practicing the slow version) is that you can use it to turn all of your systems online, so to speak, meaning you feel fully aware and present in your body, ready to tackle any task.

Initiating Ritual

The Witch Heart sets us into motion, marking the rhythm of the days and seasons, the cycles of life, and the dance of the moon and sun across the sky. It helps us celebrate the big moments and embrace every breath in between them. So how do we create ritual that best reflects our practice?

Figuring out ritual can be a bit like "Goldilocks and the Three Bears" meets "Little Red Riding Hood": *This ritual is too long and dry, but that one was too short and erratic. This ritual doesn't have any teeth, while that ritual is too intense for what it's supposed to do. Ah, this ritual is just right!* I should also state that no bears, wolves, grandparents, or children should be harmed in the course of your ritual.

Ritual should have a purpose and it should have a result. That may seem obvious, but I have observed far too many rituals where the purpose was never defined, and it essentially never achieved anything besides occupying time. How is that possible? When people get too hung up on the details, such as props, costuming, and sticking to a long script, they can stifle the flow of the ritual. Some people do a ritual because they feel that's what they're "supposed" to do, but they lack any sort of goal or focus. Then there are folks who are afraid to invest in the ritual actually working, so they basically self-sabotage and the ritual falls flat.

If you first consider what kind of ritual you are seeking to do, the pattern will start to fall in place. There is a purpose and therefore there is a guideline to follow.[7] Ritual enhances patterns but also enables you to break them when needed. They can celebrate consistency or initiate change.

The kinds of rituals we do tend to fall under one or more of the following categories:

- *Contingent/Initiatory:* Centers on personal transition, need, or crisis
- *Ancestral/Devotional:* Honors the deceased, deities, or spirits
- *Divinatory/Revelatory:* For divining and revealing
- *Protective/Preventive:* Ensures the health and safety of people, land, animals, etc.
- *Seasonal/Cyclical:* Oriented to a moment in the lunar or solar cycle

---

7. For even more information about designing ritual, please see pages 124–129 of my book *Weave the Liminal: Living Modern Traditional Witchcraft* (Woodbury, MN: Llewellyn, 2019).

For example, an initiation or elevation within a tradition would be a contingent ritual. A healing ritual for someone severely ill would be both contingent and protective. Scrying with the full moon would be a divinatory and cyclical ritual. A ritual to call upon the Mighty Dead might be both an ancestral and a protective ritual. If you do a ritual for Imbolc and it focuses on the goddess Brigid, then it's a devotional and seasonal ritual. Some of these rituals might be done on a regular basis, every year, or only happen one time ever, depending on the need and purpose.

To establish a pattern of practice with ritual, consider what you'd like to focus on. If you're looking to build a daily practice, then you'll want to start simple and small. Trying to do something elaborate and lengthy every day can be exhausting, even if you might have the time for it. Here are just a few suggestions to get your cauldron bubbling.

Ideas for Daily Ritual

- Focusing on a daily intention while making your morning brew
- Honoring your body during a morning or evening bath/shower
- Observing life in your neighborhood while walking the dog
- Pulling a tarot or oracle card, rune, or bone every day
- Working in the garden for fifteen minutes
- Anointing yourself with an oil or perfume to focus your day
- A nightly gratitude meditation

Ideas for Weekly Ritual

- Tidying and refreshing an altar
- Designate one day a week to dance or focus on ritual movement
- Cook a special meal for yourself/the spirits/a community gathering
- Sweep/wash and bless your entryway/front door
- Do a full-scale divinatory reading on your past week or the week to come
- Volunteer/be of service in your local community

Ideas for Monthly Ritual

- Esbat observation (lunar-oriented ritual; can be on a new moon, full moon, or other moon phase of your choosing)
- A monthly sigil crafting to direct energy for the upcoming month
- A day set aside just for focused craft studies
- Reconnect with/honor genius loci, house spirit, ancestor, etc.

Ideas for Yearly Ritual

- Recognizing the beginning (or end) of a season
- Marking the birthday of a deceased ancestor
- Honoring a feast day of a saint or spirit
- Celebrating a sabbat or regional festival

All of the rituals will likely look and feel completely different, with the common factor being you. Ritual will vary from Witch to Witch, flavored by their path, focus, background, and location. Don't compare yourself to what you might hear or see others doing (especially online). How your ritual feels matters more than how it may physically look. Remember, ritual can be very elaborate or simple—as long as it works for you.

Structure-Wise, Ritual Can Be:

Formal Ordered Solitary	Informal Planned Theatrical Rehearsed	Impromptu Tradition-oriented Participatory Invisible	Ecstatic One-time only Organic

Purposes and Energetic Flows for Rituals

To collect/gather	To exchange	To finish
To balance	To communicate	To uncover/reveal
To transform	To protect	To acknowledge
To cleanse	To heal	To celebrate
To build	To start	To remember/honor

Whether you plan a ritual in advance or it happens in the moment, there is a consistent design flow among effective rituals:

Start ➤ Build ➤ Sustain ➤ Climax ➤ Completion

Start

Every ritual should have a clear start to mark the beginning. This can be as simple as taking a breath, ringing a bell, lighting a candle or incense, or announcing your intention. If you are working alone, this focuses your mind and marks that you are shifting space. If you are working with other people, it's vital to have everyone on the same page.

Build

Build can refer to both metaphysically and physically preparing a space, depending on your needs. This includes creating a magic circle, aligning your body, or laying out tools, ingredients, or other components.

Sustain

Once the ritual has begun and everything is in order, it's time to get on with the purpose of your ritual and achieving your desired result. This may look like singing, chanting, dancing, drumming, or another desired activity/interaction.

Climax

The climax of the ritual is where the peak purpose is set in motion or achieved. It is the communing with deities or spirits, sending off healing energy, divining or scrying, or some other form of desired connection.

Completion

Just as you clearly started the ritual, you should mark its end. Again, this could be something as simple as how you started (with a breath or utterance), or it could be breaking down what has been built. It also includes ritual aftercare of the self, others, the space, etc. Always clean up after yourself.

Remember:

- It's okay to laugh and have fun.
- Don't be afraid to make a mistake. The world will not end, and the ritual may work out better than planned.
- Work with the flow, not against it.
- Consider safety and well-being in advance. Be prepared!
- Keep your purpose in mind.
- Less is often more.
- Trust in yourself.
- Things usually take longer than you expect.
- Clean up after yourself, physically and metaphysically.

Ritual is weaving the liminal. In these various states and actions, you are able to sense the connections of spirit, place, and being, and work with them. The metaphysical and the practical become partnered, and your own sense of the pattern that you are both a part of and weave is strengthened.

Muscle Memory

When it comes to the body, some muscles do their job with little effort on our part. The heart is a muscle that does its work without us ever consciously thinking about it. The process is automatic, but the rhythm of our breathing can speed up our heartbeat or slow it down. Other muscles need our mental guidance and focus to perform their tasks. In addition, they require regular exercise to maintain good health and strength and to develop skill for maximum efficiency.

Not unlike muscles, you have metaphysical tools you can consciously use at your fingertips, and there are some practices that function better at the subconscious or even unconscious level. Rituals that are part of your daily routine often become automatic in nature. You likely are not consciously thinking every morning, "I clean my teeth to promote good health, I wash my body to smell pleasing, I apply moisturizer to support my skin..." You're actually more likely thinking about the coming day or what you said last night, or what you're going to have fun doing that evening. But still that process of ritual happens while your mind wanders—its impact not lessened by whatever else your mind may be focusing on. You've developed what folks tend to refer to as "muscle memory."

Then there are the activities that you will do where you must be wholly present to reap the maximum benefits: initiations, dedications, consecrations, seasonal rites, etc. Ecstatic workings that involve trance require a full commitment, despite the fact that you might feel like you're not consciously present. But even with those active workings—if you have done them enough times—there's a sense of muscle memory at play. For example, if there is a poem that is always recited, or a common response to an invocation or evocation, there's a good chance you'll automatically respond because that's part of the established pattern.

Think about your processes for performing rituals, spellcraft, and other workings. What kinds feel like second nature to you, and what kinds take work? Where is your comfort/discomfort zone, and what do you think that means for your practice? For example, I am extremely comfortable performing ecstatic ritual and creating things in the moment. I am far less comfortable working with scripts and having to memorize orders of actions. I could avoid the latter all together, but I've taken it upon myself to work with another group whose rites are largely composed of preserved traditions. I am absolutely not in my comfort zone, but I consider it an excellent challenge and a chance to grow my experiences. Comfort is a lovely thing, but choosing an opportunity for growth can be the greater teacher.

Witchcraft requires strength of mind, body, and spirit, and the use of ritual can help build those. Physical, mental, and emotional discipline is developed over time with practice and experiences—both good and bad. We tend to focus only on successes and give value to what we perceive as positive. But things we see as negative can also help us significantly in the long run. If we do not have challenges to overcome and problems to solve, we may not be as resilient as we think we are. Rather than letting past mistakes flood you with shame and regret, use them as tools for making better, more educated actions in the future. Consider how vaccines work. Exposure to a virus on a minimal level helps our immune system develop antibodies so we don't get sick from that virus in the future. If we suffer a physical injury like a sprain or broken bone, then after a period of rest, we must work to strengthen that area. The hard part is respecting the whole journey and being patient with ourselves.

Practice Makes Power

You may still be wondering, "But is daily practice and ritual all that? What do I really get from it?" I want to share with you something I learned as this book came into being. In March of 2020, the entire planet came to a standstill as we tried to deal with the COVID-19 virus across the globe. The resulting pandemic interrupted events, festivals, and gatherings of all sorts, majorly impacting my own busy travel schedule, which centered around teaching and performing. Many magical practitioners felt out of sorts without their weekly or monthly coven/group meetings, festivals, classes, and other regular things to help ground and drive their paths. Lots of folks figured this couldn't last too long, so instead of initiating new patterns, they opted to just wait it out. But things didn't get back to normal in a few weeks or even a couple of months. Even though I enjoy working with other people and missed traveling, I've always been fairly self-sufficient in my personal practice. But about six months into the pandemic, the lack of being on the move regularly was truly wearing me down inside and out.

I really needed to physically move my body more and to be able to do it within my own home. But that something also had to be engaging in mind and spirit too. So I decided I would start doing something on a daily basis that got me moving and had a magical theme to it. I would then record it to video and post the result on YouTube. I dubbed my YouTube channel the *Witchual Workout*. The term *witchual* originated in one of my usual on-the-spot verbal creations during a workshop several years ago, when my brain was moving faster than my mouth (which happens when I'm excited). I had already started to include the term in this book, so that seemed to be a good idea to build upon. I figured that if I put the videos online for others to follow, it would help to hold me accountable to do the thing on a regular basis. I also wanted to make them adjustable to fit a wide variety of levels of ability and mobility, and especially accessible to folks who may be intimidated by dance. The last detail is that each video would be a single take, unedited, nothing fancy.

I started off recording a video every single day with the following themes, with each episode lasting generally between eight to fifteen minutes:

- *Monday:* Lunar work
- *Tuesday:* Oracle/tarot pull
- *Wednesday:* Deities/spirits
- *Thursday:* Oracle/tarot pull
- *Friday:* Free choice (whatever inspires me that day)
- *Saturday:* Spellwork
- *Sunday:* Solar work

At forty episodes in, I realized that seven days a week was too much for me. I needed to take a couple days' break mentally to recharge and rest. So the weekend themes got incorporated into the other days as seemed appropriate to the day. Nearly every video has a warm-up, a goal, and a means of creating sacred space that varies, so there's always something new to think about or learn.

The biggest thing I noticed about these videos was that besides getting me to move more and improving my headspace, there were some other powerful effects as well. My connection to my practice deepened, and I started to notice even more patterns revealing themselves. The workouts themselves developed their own weekly themes and correlations, which related to what was happening in the larger world as well. This project heightened my sense of connection—not only to my body, but also to the world around me. In posting the videos for others to enjoy, I helped others with their own practice and built community as well. All this for an activity that generally takes just ten to twenty minutes of my day, five days a week.

I'm now well past a hundred episodes on the playlist. I'll keep doing them as long as I feel the need to and posting them for folks to enjoy. The archives can be found at my YouTube channel: https://www.youtube.com/c/Laura ZakroffWitch.

So if you're looking to deepen your magical practice, to feel more truly connected as a Witch, then I can't recommend a daily practice enough. Find something small that you can reliably spend some regular time doing. Look back at the list of daily suggestions earlier in this chapter. Just start doing it. Don't be too hard on yourself if you need to shift the pace or change how you do things. Remember, it's not the individual acts that matter so much, but rather the consistency of doing the small things on a regular basis that brings the greatest effect. Listen to your heart and let it guide you.

Heart Vision: The Eye of the Beholder

The Witch Heart, a human heart with a single eye in it, is a common motif in my artwork. Why the eye in the heart? What does this symbol mean? Art often depicts things that cannot so easily be put into words, but I will try.

I feel the eye in the heart is able to perceive some things that our physical eyes may not be capable of. It's a kind of internal vision that sees more clearly than our actual eyes, more precisely than what our brains can process. For example, we talk about the idea of love at first sight—but that's not necessarily something we sort out logically in our heads. Rather, we are typically overcome by a sensation in our chest: excitement, nervousness, exhilaration, desire, longing, and other difficult-to-pin-down emotions. These feelings are different from gut instinct, which we'll dive into in the next chapter. They tend to override both mental logic and survival presets. Love is like shifting into another gear you didn't even know you had. It can be powerful, even overwhelming. Even though we may not be able to use logic to reason out why we feel that way, we know whatever we feel in our heart to be true and reliable. That is the vision the Witch Heart can grant.[8]

The eye itself is a motif we find again and again around the world and throughout history. Our ancestors recognized that the world is more than simply what we can visually see. The eye can symbolize deities, spirits, angels, protection, guidance, mystery, and psychic vision. The eyes are frequently described as the window (or mirror) of the soul. When we see "eye to eye," there is a sense

---

8. Check out "Witchual Workout 114: Heart Vision Meditation" on my YouTube channel, https://www.youtube.com/watch?v=MWn8un43J78.

of mutual understanding and equality. Two or more Witch Hearts gathered together can bring about tremendous group work and manifestations.

Encapsulated within the symbolism of the eye is the fact that we are seeing as well as being seen. We observe similarities and differences, grouping like things together and separating out those that don't match. Knowing that we are also being watched by the world around us (as we watch it), we seek to control how, when, and where we are seen. We put up walls and curtains and obscure that which we don't wish to reveal or prefer to keep hidden. Put into plain speak like that, it may seem like we're up to nefarious things, but a desire for privacy and even secrecy is built into our brains. We don't have to necessarily wear our heart on our sleeve for all to see, but rather keep it close to us.

Not everything has to be out in the open or on display. There is power in keeping some things to ourselves. In the realm of Witchery, choosing what we wish to reveal and what is secreted behind the veil can be crucial to making a ritual or working successful. Figuring out what we share and what we hide can be a difficult thing to sort out. But if we pay attention and listen to our heart and intuition, we may find it's not as hard as we think.

☾ WITCHUAL ☽
Elemental Hearts

A veritable cauldron of emotions, the Witch Heart can feel immersed in different elements at times. We might even perceive an elemental-leaning heart in someone else. As mentioned in the introduction, every element has traits we admire and others we may not be so fond of. Here are some ways of looking at the element-immersed Witch Heart:

- *Heart of Air:* Breath, movement, lightness, transparent, flighty, ungrounded, fickle
- *Heart of Fire:* Passion, consume, purify, inspiring, explosive, temperamental
- *Heart of Water:* Incubate, replenish, cleanse, drown, full of emotion, flood
- *Heart of Earth:* Growth, opaque, garden (overgrown or tended to), compost

Right at this moment, which element does it feel like your heart is most closely connected to, and how does that make you feel? Does this feel to be something in a mutable, fixed, or cardinal state? If you feel it needs improvement (cleansing, weeding, dusting, etc.), think about how would you go about doing that ritually. Would it be a physical task you could do that is sympathetic in nature, such as taking a cleansing bath, weeding the garden, or cleaning your living room? Or perhaps a meditation, trance working, or some artful exploration? What if you were to choose something from each element to place on your altar in a heart shape that creates a new mixture that is inspiring for you? There is no right or wrong answer, but simply what works for that moment in time—and there's a good chance it will work again. Keeping track of what yields the most effective results will help create stronger patterns in your practice. But don't be afraid to experiment as well, especially if you feel stuck after a while.

Here are some ideas to get you moving:

- *Heart of Air:* Here's an easy one to do if you need to clear out ideas that make your heart feel heavy. With a cleansing smoke wand, draw the shape of a heart in the air outside, and visual those weighty thoughts dispersing in the wind. Be sure to check which way the wind is blowing first.

- *Heart of Fire:* If you'd like to create interest or excitement for something, place a representation of that something (a picture, word, or object) at the center of a heart-shaped ring of tealight candles during the waxing or full moon.

- *Heart of Water:* If you're looking to slow something down, consider carving a heart into an ice cube, and keep it frozen. Inversely, you could use water to draw a heart on a hot surface to sizzle if you're looking to heat up a situation.

- *Heart of Earth:* There's something so nice and comforting about holding a heart-shaped stone—and they often fit nicely into a pocket or purse. Carry a hematite heart to ward off negativity or a quartz heart to promote clarity.

Elemental Hearts

Be Still, Breath and Blood

Our Witch Lungs and Heart work together to keep us moving, but is there room for quiet, calm, and stillness?

Think about the meaning behind the expression "holding my breath." This phrase suggests there is a sense of anticipation or suspense, possibly out of fear or excitement. Prey animals (like rabbits) freeze when they perceive danger. There's a sense of the fight-or-flight response—to be prepared for anything to happen. Small children often threaten to hold their breath until they get their desired result. It's actually pretty hard to do, because our bodies want to breathe. We'll pass out before any harm comes to us. We also hold our breath while swimming underwater for short amounts of time—to be able to check out another world below the surface or swim undetected. We might have been told when we were little to hold our breath as we passed a cemetery so that the dead don't get jealous or follow us. If we're decidedly *not* holding our breath about something, it means we don't expect something to happen at all—that it's unlikely or improbable.

In Witchcraft practice, we might look at these expressions in an altogether different way. We might withhold our breath so that we're not lending energy or input to something we don't want to be a part of (for our benefit or perhaps the benefit of others). We might hold our breath to create a pause, adding extra focus and intention to whatever we choose to do next. We might use it to interrupt an unhealthy or undesirable pattern, such as becoming angry or anxious over something. We may "take a breather" to create a space or break from something we usually do. We use breathing techniques to achieve a state of calm and collectedness.

Sometimes you are working more against your own well-being versus accomplishing whatever you think you're setting out to do. If you're feeling overwhelmed by your practice, take a breather and step back for a little while. Just as there is power in movement, there is also power in stillness. As the dust settles, try to objectively examine your work. Have you been fighting the current rather than going with the flow?

A simple exercise you can do when feeling stressed is to first do the 3 Breaths. Next put a hand over your heart so that you can feel it beating. Breathe in while slowly counting 1, 2, 3, 4. Then exhale slowly while counting 4, 3, 2, 1. Focus only on the sensation of your heartbeat, your breath, and the count of four. Repeat for three cycles, then remove your hand from your chest. Inhale sharply through your nose and exhale loudly through your mouth, releasing your shoulders as you breathe out.

Witch Heart Sigil

After spending some time with the Witch Lungs Sigil, it's time to move on to the Witch Heart. Use this sigil as a meditational or ritual focus for helping you find the pattern of your Witch Heart. You could carve it on a candle, draw it for your altar, or anoint it on your chest. Begin with the 3 Breaths and recite the poem at the beginning of this chapter, then allow inspiration to flow. If you have access to a light drum, you can use it to gently beat a heartbeat rhythm. If you need to be more quiet or aren't into percussive instruments, find a song with a good rhythm and slip on some headphones. Focus on the beat and how it makes you feel.

Witch Heart Sigil

Chapter 3

The Serpent

Deep in the belly, nestled in our core,
A serpent moving from sky to floor.
Primal yet sensual, ancient and wise,
Knowing the secrets apart from lies.
Renew, transform, slither, shedding skin,
Protecting and freeing soul within.

When the Serpent speaks, it reveals the truth of ourselves. It's not the world that needs "rewilding" or "re-enchanting." It's us—or more specifically, the parts of ourselves that have disconnected from our own natural powers.

The Serpent is the most primal part of ourselves—it's not like a patch of earth that can be colonized and contained to fit behind white picket fences. It is wild, wise, fluid, and often full of surprises. While we may not understand it at the time, the Serpent is often our best alarm system, warning us about potential dangers or things to pay attention to.

The Serpent can dive deep, seemingly hibernate, and then suddenly emerge out of nowhere, without warning. It can seem perfectly content, languidly resting in the sun, and then become disturbed or unsettled. The Witch listens to the primal self within, striking a balance between action and rest.

The Serpent says, "Kiss the air with your tongue, move your body like water, let your spirit burn like fire, and glide upon the earth with ease."

The Empress

Be abundant and complete within yourself.

The Priestess sets you on the path, creating patterns for you to uncover and work with. Many of these processes become like clockwork; they set the pace and further emphasize your space and abilities. They make a shelter or working space for the next level of work—to allow your subconscious and unconscious levels to bubble up to the surface.

The Empress has walked through the mysteries of the Priestess and now sits upon her throne to observe the world around her. She nurtures creativity and fertility and promotes abundance. She offers healing waters but also protects those she nurtures with fierceness. The Empress has been known to do a dance or twelve in her time, but she also doesn't mind sitting still. She is not afraid of reinventing herself, but she also honors spirit in every form taken. The Empress is all about considering choices and having the power to make decisions.

The Witch Heart has led you here to explore your emotions and learn to listen to your intuition. Come have a drink with the Empress and sit a spell to learn about power and choice. Choose to have a conversation with the Serpent.

Finding the Serpent

Cradled within your pelvis, a serpentine energy is coiled, biding its time. For some, the Serpent represents all that is wrong with the earthly realm: sin, temptation, slithery things. But prior to some relatively recent bad publicity, the snake has long been honored as a creature of wisdom. Serpent energy can reveal to you the mysteries of rebirth, healing, and transformation.

Also located in your lower body cavity are your intestines, which can certainly look like a nest of snakes. When we talk about instinct and intuition, you might wonder why the phrase "follow your gut" or "I had a gut feeling" comes up so often. Folks commonly associate being psychic with the mind—so central to the head—yet here we are talking about the belly. There is actual science behind it, as your intestinal lining is home to a large number of neurons that communicate with your brain via the vagus nerve. The vagus nerve runs from the base of the brain, through the chest, and down into the abdomen. The base of the brain is often referred to as the reptilian brain, as it controls our most basic life functions and survival behaviors. So that "gut feeling" is the Serpent using that ancient communication system to keep us alert and prepared. I find that this intuition is rarely wrong, even if I might not know why I'm heeding it in the moment. Survive first, thrive later, right?

The Serpent also taps into your most carnal, animalistic energy. The most basic process of life is to reproduce—from asexual single-celled organisms to herbs and trees to rabbits and us. There is clearly more to human life than procreating, so keep in mind that you should not limit yourself to that box. Your work can be fertile with creativity and generate a legacy not unlike biological progeny. Also, you can be sensual without being sexual. You can be sexual without being procreative.

Encapsulated within the Serpent are aspects of both male- and female-oriented symbolism: yes, snakes can remind us of phalluses, with their long, lithe forms and shaped heads, but there's also the *ouroboros*, the snake that consumes itself, often depicted in art as forming an oval or circle as it eats its tail. In Hinduism, the word *Kundalini* (meaning coiled snake in Sanskrit) describes a divine feminine energy that rests at the base of the spine—which is present in all genders. The Orphic Egg from Greek mythology is often depicted as a large egg with a serpent wrapped around it. From this primordial egg the hermaphroditic deity Phanes/Protogonus was hatched, who in turn created the other deities that populated the world. Prognosis? The Serpent is gender-fluid.

Knowing that the snake is so primal and powerful, it's not surprising it has been so maligned, especially by societies that espouse puritanical and restricted ideas about sex, gender, and identity. We are still dealing today with social restraints and cultural taboos, such as "sex should only be between a married man and woman" and "sex is for reproductive purposes only—but also, masturbation is a sin." How limiting, boring, and completely ignorant of the diversity and powers of the human body! There's also the whole array of different levels and labels of sexuality that can send conservative minds spinning: asexual, demisexual, bisexual, pansexual, homosexual, heterosexual, and more. Sex magic can be powerful stuff, and worth exploring in the right situations either by yourself or consensually with a partner (or partners). But there are other ways to connect with Serpent energy as well, so don't let anyone fool you into believing sex magic is the only way. If you view the world through a magically inclined lens, then everything from cooking to showering to fucking can have a magical expression to it. I have had incredible visions during sex that I've later used in my artwork. But I've also had similar visions when I'm on the brink of falling asleep, taking a shower, or dancing. What that says to me is that there is likely a common mental state or focus achieved during all of these physical activities that tickles the right spot in my brain. The Serpent speaks in many ways. To be clear, you don't need to be sexually active or interested to work with the Serpent, nor do your sex organs need to be intact or present in your body. You are still home to the Serpent regardless.

When I'm instructing folks on basic dance posture, one of the most important areas I focus on is the pelvic region. As we've already seen, there are a lot of things going on in this area that align with the Serpent. Working with the pelvis can open up new sensations and increase control over your lower organs and muscles. It can also be a gateway for healing trauma (physical or emotional). I remember a dance instructor years ago mentioning that so much emotional baggage is held within the hips, and that it isn't uncommon for folks to find themselves crying when they start to work in those areas—not from physical pain, but from unlocking subconscious parts of their brain that have been lying in the shadows for years. Afterward there is generally a huge sense of release and relief from working those areas. Doing low-impact exercises that activate your hips on a regular basis may help you tackle emotional and mental trials more effectively, preventing emotional constipation and other tension.[9]

Hiss...

The Serpent has some things to say, so listen up:

Your magic is not rooted in your reproductive organs, gender, or sexuality. Magic can certainly happen in and with those organs, but don't be confined by

---

9. I find it difficult to safely instruct hip movements via book format, otherwise I would include some exercises here. I do have an instructional video available called *DecoDance: Nouveau Noir Bellydance* that guides you through this area as well as the rest of your body (available at my website, https://lauratempestzakroff.com). You can also look me up on YouTube.

those roles. Being able to bring forth life is an amazing thing, but to associate your magic or identity strictly with reproductive organs is reducing all people to parts. This limited way of thinking does not actually empower anyone for long. The less you associate the effectiveness and use of your reproductive organs with your identity and capability for magic, the better.

You don't have to be assigned female at birth to call down or invoke a goddess.

You don't have to be assigned male at birth to call down or invoke a god.

You don't need to have a heterosexual or heteronormative coupling to enact the Great Rite or draw down the sun/moon.

You don't need to participate in the gender binary to work magic. You have everything you need.

Just don't step on snek.

The Sacred Serpent

All throughout world mythology, you will find evidence of the Serpent. It is truly one of the oldest symbols known to humanity, spanning themes of wisdom, healing, death, transformation, protection, immortality, and fertility. Here is a sampling of some snakelore.

Guardians and Protection

Many temples and sacred sites are guarded by serpents. The Gorgons in Greek mythology (remember Medusa) were originally associated with protecting temples. In the home, both Hestia (Greek) and Aspelenie (Slavic) are hearth goddesses who have been said to appear in the form of a small snake.

Serpents often guard the world trees of their mythologies, including Veles in Slavic myths, Níðhöggr in Norse stories, and the Vision Serpent from Mayan legend.

Wadjet, in her cobra form, is the protector of Egypt (as seen in the crowns of pharaohs) as well as an oracle possessing the all-seeing eye of wisdom.

Health and Medicine

Asclepius (or Asklepios), the Greek god of medicine and healing, carries a staff with one serpent wrapped around it.

Mami Wata (Western/Central/Southern Africa and diaspora) brings fertility and healing. She is generally shown as a woman holding a very large snake or as a half-woman, half-serpent being.

Underworld and Divination

The Oracle at Delphi was known as the Pythia, which harkens back to Python, a serpent being that guarded the navel of the world and was slain by Apollo. The oracle and temple then fell under his domain.

In ancient Egypt, Nehebkau, a two-headed serpent deity, guards the entrance to the Underworld.

The caduceus is a winged wand or staff encircled by two serpents wielded by the Greek god Hermes, who is an emissary and messenger of the gods, able to move quickly between the mortal and divine realms. Hermes also acts as a psychopomp by guiding souls to the next life. In his hands, the caduceus represents balanced exchange and dual powers—able to give or take life, to bring sleep or cause someone to awaken.

Creation

Damballah is an important spirit of creation in Haitian Vodou and Louisiana Voodoo traditions. He is represented as a great pure white serpent who connects the worlds. His wife, Ayida-Weddo, is called the Rainbow Serpent. (She is not to be confused with the Rainbow Serpent of Australian mythology.) Together they balance the forces that make life on Earth possible.

In Australian Dreamtime lore, the Rainbow Serpent created the universe, and its undulations gave rise to the mountains and valleys. Its gender varies from group to group, ranging from male to female to hermaphroditic. It is also associated with healing.

While we no longer know the exact mythology behind its creation, the 1,348-foot-long Great Serpent Mound rests in Ohio. Sculpted from the earth and swallowing an egg, the serpent's head aligns with the summer solstice. (I highly recommend a visit if you happen to find yourself in Ohio.)

Serpent Wisdom

The Serpent encompasses so many different qualities: creation, psychic vision, renewal, healing, protection, and more. They may seem unrelated, but these powers are all nested within the Serpent for good reason—they are paths to wisdom. Here are some ways you can connect with each of them.

Creation

The Empress is both a creator and a patron of the arts. In many myths, the serpent's body gives way to make a new creation or reality. You don't need to meet your own demise to create something amazing, but all creation does involve sacrifice. Things that are worthwhile making require a certain amount of your time, energy, and material resources. This means as a creator, you must give yourself credit and respect for your work. As a patron, if the work is something you desire, then it has value and the creator deserves respect and proper support.

Vision

See and listen with the whole of your body. To hear the Serpent requires an investment in silence: to say no to the things that demand your attention without giving anything back, to the voice that insists on speaking over everything.

Become stillness. You don't have to "quiet" or "empty" your mind. This is an invitation to slow down—to hold the moment, savor the air, listen to the silence, and simply be. Don't worry about what's next or where you should be or need to be. Where you are at this moment is the right place to be. Let things wash over you like the waves of a lake, slowly breaking, returning, cycling, refreshing. There will be visions of perfect clarity and there will be times when things become turbulent and the waters will be muddy, difficult to see what lies beneath. This isn't a failing: it's natural. Not all visions make sense right away. Sometimes you must sit with them before the truth is revealed.

Renewal and Healing

Snakes have earned the reputation of rebirth because they shed their skin by sloughing off the old one. It is not always an easy process for them either. Shedding makes them vulnerable, and sometimes they need a little help.

Shedding for you can mean releasing ideas and things that are harmful to you, whether they originate in others or yourself. Letting go of blame, shame, and other negative emotions, discharging body dysmorphia, removing abusive people in your life—these are all things to shed. The process may seem scary or potentially painful, and it may even require some professional help, but it will give way to healing. When you heal, you make yourself new.

Movement can also be incredibly healing, not just movement of the body but also of the mind. The Zaar from Northern Africa and the Tarantata from Italy are both folkloric trance dances that use vigorous movement to heal the heart and mind. Their folklore may attribute the malediction to spirit possession or the bite of a spider, respectively, but the root of the actual issue is usually extreme repression of the mind and the sexual nature present in the culture. We may see ourselves a bit more liberated, but that doesn't discount the power of getting up and moving your body. You don't need to stage a performance or an elaborate ritual to move your body. Put on some songs that get the Serpent inspired and let loose.

Protect

"There is no good offense without a solid defense" tends to be a message in most sports-oriented movies. Translation from the Serpent point of view: "If you're going to strike out into the world or otherwise put yourself out there, take some precautions. Remember to summon your sovereign self, and a little extra magical charm doesn't hurt either. Having something you put on that has protective shielding as you get out in the world can go a long way, whether it's a symbol of deity or power, an invisible sigil, or an evil eye bracelet.

The majority of snakes aren't venomous, but some have evolved to have characteristics that are visually similar to the venomous ones, effectively scaring off potential predators. Be the danger noodle.

Beware the Venom

It's vital to know how to protect yourself (and others) and stand your ground when necessary. That includes knowing which battles to engage in and which you should walk away from. It also means keeping your ego in check and not letting power get to your head. Keep this in mind when dealing with other magical practitioners.

Some folks think that once they've claimed their space, lined up all of the tools, and ticked off the ritual boxes, they're masters. Yet you'll likely see them having tantrums and emotional breakdowns that would put toddlers to shame. Their work is unstable and erratic, even though it may seem impressive on the surface. They have not engaged with the Serpent. Avoid them when possible.

The Water Serpent: Cleansing and Purifying

While we often think of the snake as a creature of earth or fire, water can be its home as well. Watching a snake swim is fascinating and entrancing—they just seem to skim across the surface, leaving serpentine ripples in their wake. Then there are the sea serpents of lore, whose bodies are only hinted at when they break the surface, appearing for just a brief moment. So many more mysteries can await below, lurking in untold depths. The element of Water can provide a place of contemplation, revelation, and wonder, both above and below. Our own Serpent needs some time to tap into the rejuvenating powers of Water.

Cleansing and purification are ways we can renew and refresh the Serpent. While everything the body does is natural, that doesn't mean it doesn't get dirty or accumulate toxins or other impurities—especially in a spiritual context. Cleansing and purification are especially helpful when we are experiencing stressful situations, are encountering things that make us feel unwell or uneasy, or want to spiritually make a new start or transition.

Every culture has a prescription for cleansing the body, which usually involves incorporating one or more of the following elements: steam, smoke, salt, water, or earth. There are wet and dry saunas, sweat lodges, mikveh (Jewish), hamman (Arabic), banya (Russian), hot and cold tubs, rooms made of salt, sand, or charcoal, and so forth. There are common themes that come up again and again around the globe for these bathing practices. Depending on the culture, baths may be recommended after menstruation and childbirth, before or after sexual activity, before sacred holidays and special events, before or during sacraments, before or during spiritual evolution (initiation, conversion), and after death.

Baths can be communal or solitary experiences. In cultures that encourage communal bathing (whether separated by gender or not), there tends to be greater acceptance and appreciation of the body—and typically less of a taboo about being naked. There is something beautiful and amazing about seeing a wide range of body shapes and the effects of aging. Every single body is unique. When you see other people's bodies up close and personal in a nonsexual context, there is a sense of familiarity. When our main opportunity to view other bodies is filtered through Photoshop on magazine pages and media screens, we get a false sense of what our bodies are naturally meant to look like.

Keep this in mind the next time you examine your body in the bathroom mirror. Your body is a beautiful creation, made up of real experiences that are reflected in and under your skin.

☾ WITCHUAL ☽
Ritual Baths

If you don't have a giant personal cauldron (aka a bathtub), you can modify these baths to work in the shower as well. You can also integrate a smoke cleansing with your favorite incense before or after a ritual bath.

Mugwort Rinse

I don't get to go to a spa often, but one of my favorites has a font of mugwort-infused water. They provide large bowls and the idea is to scoop the water up and pour it over your body, like a self-applied shower. Mugwort (Artemisia vulgaris) is magically used for enhancing psychic vision and aiding in protection. It is a very common and inexpensive herb that grows practically everywhere, so it's easy to obtain. The easiest and least messy way to use it is to make an infusion. Collect the dried herb in a muslin satchel or tea bag—enough to fill the bag. Add to a large pot of bath-safe-temperature water for at least five minutes. Then pour it into your bath or use in the shower. (Warning: Mugwort is not suitable for pregnant or lactating women. It should not be used for daily baths, but only once in a while for special occasions.)

Rosemary Venik

Rosemary is another easy and inexpensive herb to acquire that has an array of magical uses. It can be used for enhancing memory, building strength, invigorating the spirit, providing protection, and cleansing. In Russian bathhouses, a venik is a broom usually made of oak branches used in a vigorously percussive-like massage. It warms up and invigorates the body. Taking inspiration from that practice, you can gather fresh rosemary sprigs into a small spray (four to six twigs, each about seven to eight inches long). While in the bath or shower, gently yet vigorously tap your body with the rosemary broom (avoiding your eyes and delicate bits). You should be able to smell the wonderful aroma and feel refreshed.

Preserving and Building Energy

When I ask folks what is the biggest obstacle to their practice, the most common issue reported is physical fatigue. The reasons behind the exhaustion or lack of energy vary as greatly as do the diverse group of people I talk to. For some, a hectic work schedule and/or family life is what consumes much of their time and energy. For others, they are navigating the aging process and feel like they can't do things the way they used to. Another leading cause is a physical ailment, a disability, or emotional problems that often hold the person back. Regardless of what's causing your fatigue, you might feel like doing ritual or other kinds of workings will just drag you down more.

One of the key problems is that so many people are taught ritual technique that depletes their reserves and leaves them feeling exhausted. At the end of most rituals, you should be feeling energized or invigorated, not wiped out. So how do you do it? The technique is twofold: it's a matter of how energy is raised in a working and then how you treat the body once you finish the work.

First it's important to understand you don't need to use up your own energy to make something work. While the body makes an excellent conduit, it sucks as a battery. Many spells involve components such as candles and herbs because those things can be like batteries, a replacement or enhancement to our own. If you understand that magic begins with thought, then you know things are already set in motion once you start thinking about what you're going to do. Sometimes, though, things are certainly helped along with a little boost. But that does not necessarily require greater physical effort on your part, if you can direct energy from around you and through you.

You are made up of atoms. Everything that is matter is essentially particles in motion—nothing is truly solid. The air we breathe is full of atoms. Anything providing illumination is bouncing particles off of you. The floor is vibrating, as is that chair, and the tablet or book you're holding right now (or the audio waves you're listening to). There is light shining from a source near you right now. All of this is potential power that you can tap into as a conduit. You can move and direct it with breath, visualization, or simple gestures of the body without even working up a sweat. Just gently touching your hands together at the fingertips creates a powerful and effective vibration. If you are in a closed room (versus the outdoors), your body will heat up the space regardless of what level of activity you're up to. What happens when molecules get heated up? They move around even more! That scientific model definitely can help you picture raising energy in a whole new way!

You can further excite the energy around you with more active movement if you are able or inspired to do so. Drumming builds power with sound, percussion (physical contact), and rhythm. Chanting and singing use sound and pattern. Dancing wakes up the body and helps it connect to its surroundings. However, with doing any of these activities, you can easily deplete your own energy source if you disconnect from the flow and purpose of the working. If you're doing the activity correctly in tune with the energy of the working, it's like standing in a stream: the water moves around you, and you can change its shape with your body. To use solely your own energy is like trying to summon spit to replace that flowing stream. As another example, if you dance to weave a pattern with other people, you're in the stream. If you dance like you're at a rave after three margaritas, you're trying to spit the stream. Remember the lesson of the Witch Lungs: breathe, focus on interconnectivity, and preserve your space.

Immersing yourself in the stream, becoming one with the presence of energy around you, is how I look at raising energy. Sticking with the water analogy here, think about walking into the ocean. When we're young, we have a tendency to just run and jump in, with no care about the temperature or where we're going. We just want to dive in! We don't care about getting wet, about catching a chill, whether our skin will get pruney, or if the current is carrying us out of reach beyond the watchful eyes of parents or lifeguards. Most of the time we're just fine, but our lack of being mindful can get us in trouble.

As we get older, we tend to become more sensitive to how warm or cool the water is, the direction of the tide, the strength of the waves, and what we might be stepping on as we go deeper. We may move out cautiously: first getting our feet wet, then wading in up to our knees and past the breakers until we're hip-deep, then finally diving in—getting completely wet. Once you're completely immersed, you are less concerned about the details and are mostly enjoying the moment with purpose, yet you are still keeping an eye out for jellyfish and not letting the tide sweep you out. You might do a backstroke, surf, snorkel, or just float along, depending on how calm or rough the water is. There's no sense in floating when the waves are big and choppy, nor can you surf when there are hardly any waves at all. You understand the conditions because you're in the thick of it, paying attention to the signs. You know it's time to get out when you start to feel tired or cold.

To bring us back to the process of building energy, consider the difference between the younger and the older self.[10] Each experience has its place. Children tend to have an abundance of energy, and their only motive is to play. Adults

---

10. While the ocean example uses younger you versus older you, when it comes to working with energy successfully, the depth of understanding by the individual practitioner is not determined by age or length of practice. Some people intuitively just know how to sense these things right away, and other folks will wear rituals into the ground, year after year, because they're oblivious to the current. Definitely feel free to experiment and try new things regardless of where you are in your practice. Consider why something works or doesn't work for you.

are more cautious because they've learned about potential dangers and consequences, so they're more consciously aware of their bodies. They savor the time spent and make the most of it, choosing the right activities for the conditions. As a magical practitioner building energy in a ritual or other working, you want to be focused on your goal while evaluating the situation. You want to be conscious of whether a particular method is or isn't working, so you can continue or change course as needed. Chanting doesn't seem to be having the effect you're looking for? Then maybe you should dance or light a fire instead. Be sensitive to the conditions around you, so that you're able to determine when it's time to finish the task at hand.

Directing the energy you've built up is essentially knowing when to strike, letting your Serpent intuition guide you. To take our ocean analogy one step further, this moment is spotting an incoming wave as it's coming toward you, preparing to catch it as it crests, and skillfully riding the wave all the way to the shore. Bringing the building of energy to an end is knowing when to ride that wave in. Whatever your intended goal or purpose is, that's the shoreline you're heading for. If you're doing healing work for someone, you might use a photo of them if they're not there in person with you. If you're looking to protect a place, you may walk around it or face the direction of the location if you're not local. It might be an idea you release into the sky or bury into the ground. What's most important is that you somehow make a connection (visually, mentally, physically, etc.) that helps you find your mark.

After you've raised the energy and directed it to wherever you need it to go, you're not done yet. The most crucial thing before you finish your rite, ritual, or working is that you take time to cleanse and restore the balance in your body. If you have had problems understanding the flow of energy in your body and tend to spit the stream, it's very easy to deplete yourself during the raising of energy and then drain yourself even more at the end with grounding. You've likely been to a ritual where everyone is instructed to ground at the end, which usually involves lying down on the floor and visualizing the energy coming out of you.

You're not going to find grounding like that in my rituals. First of all, unless you've figured out how to levitate, you will have been in contact with the ground the whole time through your feet. If you are properly tapped into the energy flow, then you should be able to regulate, raise, and direct energy without overexerting yourself. However, you still need to finish up with good spiritual hygiene that cleanses and replenishes you. Whether you worked with other people, spirits, planets, or the light fixtures, you directed external energy.

Engaging in ritual can be like shaking hands with a bunch of people. And after you shake a lot of hands, you definitely want to wash your hands before you do anything else. Also, while you were shaking all those hands, you were probably talking and burning some calories, so you need to hydrate and maybe have a snack. That's where spiritual hygiene comes in. It's to make sure you didn't accidentally exhaust some of your own resources or pick up anything you don't want to take with you.

✳ Exercise to Release, Replenish, and Revive ✳

Once you have reached the climax of your working, you can do the following during the completion part of your ritual.

From a standing (or sitting) position, perform the 3 Breaths exercise, focusing on the state of your body.

Next, cup your hands out in front of you but close to your body, like you're about to catch some water from a cascading waterfall.

Visualize your cup filling with pure, cool, clean water.

Raise your cupped hands just above your head, preparing to pour the "water." Visualize releasing a cleansing shower down upon you.

Slowly bring your hands apart and down in front of you, with the palms facing inward toward you and fingers gently apart as the arms are lowered.

Complete the motion until your fingertips point down toward the ground.

Repeat this movement two more times.

You can also connect each movement with the following phrases, one per cycle:

> *I release and wash away that which is not needed.*
> *I replenish that which has been absorbed.*
> *I revive and refresh myself for the work to come.*

You can also perform this exercise with an actual cup of water, though you're not going to pour it all over yourself. Instead, have a clean cup with fresh, cool water available. After doing the 3 Breaths exercise, take a swallow for each phrase, feeling the liquid go down as you drink. What's especially nice about this version is that you likely need to hydrate anyway, so you're accomplishing two vital tasks at once.

Devour Like a Snake

When we connect with the Serpent, we learn to shed our skin and when it's time to rest and time to strike. There is also symbolism to consider in how a snake takes its meals that can aid us magically. While we will look at eating and digestion more in depth in chapter 6, let's take a moment now to consider what the Serpent can teach us about it.

While snakes do have teeth, they are for biting and grasping, not chewing. Instead of chewing their food, snakes must eat their meals whole, unhinging their jaws to accommodate what they have captured—often opening much wider than their own body. Once swallowed, food slowly makes its way through their digestive track, taking quite some time to be fully absorbed by the body. Interestingly enough, the warmer the snake is, the faster it is able to digest its food.

In absorbing new information and learning new practices, you might feel like you've bitten off more than you can chew. It is easy to become overwhelmed or feel like you're not making any progress. But anything worth learning takes time and practice, especially when it comes to being a Witch. Few things are immediately evident and instantly understood on the surface. It is only when we spend time peeling back the layers, become familiar with the ingredients, and actively engage with experience that learned wisdom becomes second nature to us. Like the warm snake, the more we do, the quicker the process seems.

There are more layers of Serpent symbolism to consider as well. Recall that our own intestines are snake-like in shape, much like how the interior of our lungs resembles tree branches. Within our intestines, we are breaking down food to its bare elements, absorbing what is needed and eliminating waste, which returns to the earth. We see this vital process again and again in all individual life forms. We also know it happens collectively on the floors of forests, where insects, fungi, and microorganisms break down plant leaves and animal flesh alike. In death and decay, earth is being created and renewed. We have evolved to carry our own forest floors with us, transforming and rebuilding ourselves as well as the world.

In some myths, the Serpent is supposedly "cursed" to crawl on its belly through dirt, and even supposedly to eat it (which they don't, so weird flex there). Though if you think about it, we all eat dirt in a way, and we (human beings at least) all start off crawling. Earth is essential, receiving death and giving life—truly sacred. Crawling is part of our learning process, and we would be blessed to do it even half as elegantly and smoothly as the Serpent.

So when you find yourself frustrated with the progress of your path, put your hands on your belly and remember how the Serpent eats. Remember that you contain the mysteries of life and death within your abdomen. Transformation is just inside of you.

Following the Serpent

Traditional Witchcraft is often referred to as the "crooked path" in the sense that the journey is circuitous and winding. I find that the word *crooked* tends to bring a sense of haphazardness, being bent against one's will (something that becomes crooked because its growth has been impeded in some way), as well as tinges of dishonesty or scamming. While I have long said there is a fine line between cunning and conning when it comes to Witchcraft, this path requires you to be brutally honest with yourself. You must "know thyself" first and foremost. Of course, people can choose whatever descriptor they like to describe their path if it works for them—so if crooked works for you, great.

As for Modern Traditional Witchcraft—which combines modern practice and myth with traditional concepts and folklore—I feel there is another name that works better: the *Serpentine Path.*

The serpent is ancient, full of symbols and wisdom, yet still thrives and evolves today. A snake moves in all directions, flexing to make its way wherever it wishes. It may bend and curve to meet an obstacle, but the shape and structure of the serpent's overall being retains its integrity. It responds to environmental stimuli, but change is initiated from the inside out. The serpent is fluid, flexible, and persistent.

We also find the spiraling serpentine shapes and movement in the structure of DNA, the shape of galaxies, and the Fibonacci sequence. We ebb and flow, we rise and fall, we weave in and out, moving above and below, left and right, rushing and resting. There is a rhythm and a pattern to our paths, even if we may have difficulty spotting the motif early on.

The Serpentine Path is the work of the Weaver—the Witch who intuitively understands the patterns, both seen and unseen; whose hands work liminal threads, knowing when to add and when to discard, what to knot and cut away and what to bring in, and what to leave room for. The Weaver is able to sense things by touch, to foresee what comes ahead, while keeping an eye on the past. This Witch knows when it's time to shed everything and start anew.

Your path will have its curves and shifts. There will be times when you will want to do nothing more than lie on a rock and soak up the sun. Then there will be periods where you will need to go underground to regroup or gestate new concepts. There will be obstacles and challenges, but there will be new adventures and great wisdom to unravel. Slither on, my friends.

Serpent Sigil

Use the Serpent Sigil as a meditational focus to help you commune with your inner Serpent. Begin with the 3 Breaths exercise. With your finger, draw a serpentine line starting from your pubic bone to your chest. You may find it helpful to wet your fingertip with a favorite blessed oil or water, or consecrate some olive oil first. Recite the poem at the beginning of this chapter, then lie down, preferably oriented with your head in the west and your feet in the east. Visualize your body extending out, encompassing the globe, and relax. Pay attention to any signs, thoughts, sounds, or symbols that come to you.

Serpent Sigil

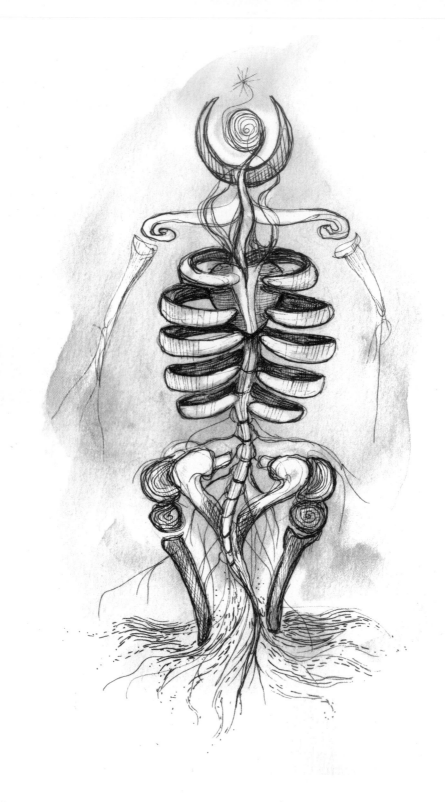

Chapter 4
Witch Bones

Breath and blood, rhythm sung in bone,
Cycle of death and life marked in stone.
Those who came before us made the mark,
Conjuring light and balancing dark.
Paths once beaten, new ones yet to tread,
What song will our bones sing once we're dead?

Oh how we Witches love our bones! We often place them on our altars, use them for divination, make them into musical instruments, and even cook them down into healing broths. We collect bones, decorate with them, and hold conversations with them. Perhaps we love them so dearly because they are artifacts of embodied spirits that have crossed the veil—those beings that once lived and breathed just as we do now, but have begun another cycle.

Skeletal remains are a reminder that death is part of life. That close association with death could explain why many people have an aversion to bones. Once our spirit has moved beyond our body, our bones may be the only physical evidence left that we existed.

Bones form the skeletal system, which maintains the structure of the body and its organs. Our bones give us shape, protect our internal organs, and aid us in mobility. As blood flows through our veins and breath expands our chest, our skeletal system is there all the while—giving our body form so we can live.

The Witch Bones give us form, structure, and strength to build our practice upon, crafting tradition. They remind us of the liminal space between life and death, bringing us the wisdom of the ancestors. Witch Bones tell us the stories that become the songs we sing in this life and carry on to the next. The Earth below our feet is made up of those who have come before us and sets the space that we share with others.

The Emperor
Standing on the shoulders of giants.

The Empress gave you insight into the most primal, intuitive, and emotional parts of yourself. Now you are rising up out of her serpentine waters to tread onto the land of the Emperor. They complement each other—for as much as the Empress is about the sensual and creative, the Emperor is about structure and stability. The number 4 is connected with balance and foundation, which is embodied in the Emperor's characteristics of being a leader and an authority figure. He reminds you where you come from—to observe tradition but not be beholden to it without reason. The Emperor protects you without confining you.

Traditions of the past provide a structure for the Witch to build a living practice upon. Witch Bones form the loom upon which you weave your practice. Without using their strong structure or if you ignore the guidelines, your work can become wobbly and skewed. The Emperor helps you to become familiar with the loom so that you can concentrate on the pattern you are weaving, in turn manifesting your dreams into reality.

The Bone Way

With the Witch Heart, we recognize how blood represents ritual pulsing through our lives. But where does blood come from? Our blood cells are actually made within our bones. So the bones create the essence that flows through our heart. In a magical sense, since bones give us structure and build our blood, Witch Bones essentially represent tradition. Our blood and bones are linked, just as the workings and practices in our path are. Blood is sustaining tradition as tradition is creating ritual. Traditions, rituals, workings, and practices—they weave together to give form to our path.

We have a tendency to think about tradition as being rigid and dry, like old bones. But in reality, tradition is more about building strength while maintaining fluidity. Tradition needs to be able to adjust with our needs, while still giving us a framework to follow. When tradition is not allowed to grow and change within reason, it can become problematic and even harmful. Consider our own bones. When we are forming in the womb, we are flexible, malleable in so many ways. Over time, much of our cartilage becomes bone, solidifying our form. Without the proper nutrients and exercise in our early development, our bones can become weak or even malformed, stunting our growth. As we get older, we are not off the hook when it comes to taking care of our bones. We still need to make sure we're getting the vitamins and exercise needed to maintain good health. We may even try new foods and hobbies as we grow older to diversify our self-care and ensure we're getting what our body needs as it changes with age.

If we consider the patterns we surround ourselves with on a daily basis, like bones they can be strong and hold us, giving us form, structure, and purpose. But our patterns can also warp us, hinder our growth, and prevent us from exploring new possibilities. Too restrictive and we miss out on opportunities and new ideas. Too open and we struggle to accomplish anything significant. Traditions can reinforce the patterns that can illuminate our path with the right balance of strength and fluidity.

In my book *Weave the Liminal*, I introduce the concept of *RITES* to help Modern Traditional Witches build authentic practices for themselves. RITES also feed into the Witch Bones, helping to give strength, structure, and direction to your practice. RITES consists of the following:

- *Roots:* Origins, myth, folklore
- *Inspiration:* Influences and leading factors
- *Time:* Seasons and schedules
- *Environment:* Location and foundation
- *Star:* Guidance, morals, and ethics

We can also align RITES with the anatomy of the Witch if we reflect upon the different components. Like the systems of our body, no one Witch body is related solely to a specific aspect. For example, Roots and Environment are both found in the Witch Bones, while Inspiration and Time can both be applied to the

Witch Heart. As you work with each aspect of the anatomy, consider where it may fit into RITES. This view can help enhance your vision of how everything is connected as you build your path.

But what if something doesn't seem right? We often can feel when something is out of place with our practice, though it may be hard to actually correct it for any number of reasons. We may trust other people's opinions more than our own gut and stick to a tradition that stifles us. We may not feel confident enough to believe we can make a difference, so we might avoid or fear making changes. Or we could reason that if we've already committed, then perhaps we can just give it a bit more time and see what happens. But sooner or later you'll figure out that you should have listened to yourself. Rather than worry about sunk costs or risk injury to your ego, it's best to move forward.

Another sticky situation can arise when we're having a disagreement about practices, particularly concerning the best way to do something. Although communication is an aspect of the Witch Lungs, these disagreements tend to stem from the Bones. The most common issue I see is static between younger and older Witches. Young Witches want to try out something new or want to find their own way, but don't want to be told they're doing it wrong. Older Witches are trying to provide guidance, but feel like they're being disrespected when they are met with resistance or told they're the ones doing it wrong. Both have good points, but neither is actually communicating—they're only hearing part of the message. Experience comes with experimentation, and strength comes from being flexible enough to always being open to new wisdom. The point where we say we know everything is when we know nothing. Both groups can benefit from learning from each other, fostering mutual respect. The best way to help each other is to say, "I see you are doing X. Can you tell me more about how or why you're doing it? I tend to approach it this way." This opens the door for tradition to build and flow in both directions.

When you're unsure if you're on the right path or doing the best thing for your practice, take a moment to evaluate the situation. Make a list of the benefits you can clearly see, as well as the potential dangers right this moment. Then consider how those things might develop moving forward. Check in with what your initial goal was and see if that's still in proper alignment. If not, then evaluate why that is the case.

✳ Aligning the Bodies ✳

Occasionally your bodies can get thrown out of alignment, both the symbolic and the physical ones. A little adjustment and a touch more awareness can shift the physical body back into alignment—which has a tendency to also help the spiritual body. I lead all of my students through a variation of the following exercise, whether I'm teaching a formal dance class or we're exploring ritual technique. I also use it for group ritual to get everyone in the same frame of mind. It can be helpful to put on some instrumental music with a slow and steady beat, or one that slowly builds up to a speed that's comfortable for you (and any other participants, if you're doing this with a group). Most importantly, listen to your body as you perform this exercise. Stop if anything feels uncomfortable or causes you pain.

To begin, start in a standing position, ideally without shoes on (socks are fine). If you're unable to stand, sitting will work too.

Perform the 3 Breaths exercise.

Focus on your feet. Rock your weight so that you shift from toes to balls to heels and back, slowly and gently. If you are in a seated position, then gently flex at your ankles to roll your feet against the floor in the same manner. It may help to consider the texture of the floor as you engage with it or wiggle your toes.

Bring your focus up from the feet to your ankles and calf muscles. Squeeze and release the muscles in your calves, feeling the strength in your lower legs.

Next softly bend and gently straighten your knees, without locking them. Let them be fluid and squishy, like the motion of the ocean. Your knees are a meeting place.

Heading up from your knees, consider the front of the thighs (the quads) and your backside (the glutes), a femur bone between each set. I find it can help to place your hands on these muscles as you flex them.

Move on up to your pelvis and allow your hips to be in a neutral position. This is accomplished by engaging your lower abdominal muscles. A simple way to locate and engage those muscles is to think about protecting your stomach from someone trying to punch it.

Check back in with the rest of your body that we've covered so far: feet, calves, knees, quads, and glutes. Then focus on your belly. Take a deep breath in and visualize your navel as a nesting place for the Serpent.

Move your focus up to your rib cage, where your sternum or breastbone is situated. The Witch Heart and Lungs are protected within. Make sure your shoulders are not hunched forward or pushed too far back. Utilize the Breathe Better technique from chapter 1 to adjust your posture for effective breath. Feel your chest expand and your heart beat as you breathe.

As you exhale, adjust your shoulders again with a little swivel or shimmy. Then starting at the elbows, move your arms out away from the body on each side (like a droopy-topped *T* or an arrow). Continue the outward motion with your wrists and extend it out to your fingertips. Bring the arms back in, relax them, and visualize settling back into the clavicles and sternum.

Next, shift your attention from your chest to your spine as it travels up through your neck and connects to your skull. Make sure your head is centered over your body—not tilted forward or relaxed too far back. Breathe in and send the air up through the top of your skull, visually reaching into the sky with the breath.

Take in the presence of your entire body, from the top of your skull all the way to the tiny bones in your feet. Breathe in again and send the breath down your spine, acknowledging the Witch Lungs, Heart, and Serpent along the way. You should feel a sense of connection from the top of your head all the way down to your feet.

You can do this exercise at the beginning of the day to reorient and awaken your body. You can also do it before you go to bed to help relieve tension and other kinds of stress you may be holding in your body.

Song of the Bones

The expression "to feel it in your bones" is to know or believe something in the very core of your being. It is more than a fleeting thought or a surface emotion. This phrase evokes a sense that something is a vital part of you—it may be the very essence of you. It can also refer to the wisdom of your heritage or ancestors coming through to you.

Do we associate bones with our ancestors because of the skeleton's ability to remain long after we have died? Or is there something to also be said about the blood of our ancestors flowing within us—made by our bones? Both are reasonable considerations. We exist because of our ancestors. Their DNA is a part of who we are, and if we have children, it will pass on to them. Research and theories about ancestral or genetic memory suggest our genes and cells may carry spirit, wisdom, and experience as well. We can turn to the Witch Bones to help us navigate and access this information, as well as make more direct contact with our ancestors.

Now, dealing with ancestors can be tricky business. You might not know your heritage, or perhaps you don't get along with your family. Your ancestors know you, even if you do not know them. You can still call to their wisdom, even if you don't know their names or origins. Don't be surprised when, after you reach out to them, some indeed introduce themselves to you and reveal more information about themselves—and, in turn, you!

For those ancestors you didn't get along with or don't believe were great people, you don't have to deal with anyone you don't want to. You can say no—to ancestors, spirits, and other entities as well. One thing to keep in mind is that it's entirely possible that those problematic deceased people might take on a different perspective on life after passing on. Transitioning to the next level, the dead can lose some attachments that held them back in life, including some of the weightier chunks of ego—gaining clearer vision about the threads that connect us all. Folks may worry about working with the spirit of a deceased loved one who might have been a devout Christian or other religion that looks down on Witchcraft. Again, I think that most spirits, after they leave their physical body, get a larger sense of how the world works beyond restrictions and previously held stereotypes. I have found this to be true with my maternal grandparents, whom I was very close to, and even the great-grandparents that I never met. They can be wonderful aids and guides in your practice.

Finding the song of our bones can help us heal past wounds and aid our own work. I'm not saying it's your job to fix your ancestors, but rather to see this work as an opportunity to build strength and gain wisdom moving forward. When it comes down to it, many of the death and ancestor rituals we do as part of our culture are more for our own benefit than for the deceased. Part of us recognizes that if we remember those who have passed on, then perhaps we too shall be remembered. The practices may become part of a tradition focused on the dead, but they serve the living just as much. We honor them, and in turn honor ourselves. There is really nothing to lose and so much to gain by opening the door to those who came before you. They already live on in your bones—why not use that strength?

✷ Call of the Bones Ritual ✷

This ritual can be used to connect with your ancestors as well as the Mighty Dead (those who have passed on whom you may not be related to but who inspire you nonetheless).

If you plan to call upon a specific ancestor or spirit, then I suggest making an altar that welcomes them. Place upon it things that they might like, such as a photo or an image of them (if you have one), something they gave you, etc. For example, if I were to call upon my grandmother, I might place the following items on the altar:

- A candle (and holder)
- A photo of my grandmother
- A piece of jewelry she gave to me
- Her favorite flower or herb
- A treat she liked to eat

- An offering of her favorite booze
- All of the above, situated on one of the linens I inherited from her

To begin, perform the 3 Breaths and create a welcoming magical space for your guest(s). Light the candle and settle down before the altar. Say the invocation that best suits whom you're looking to address (using the following two invocations as examples), then meditate before the altar or perform divination. You can also craft your invocation to address a particular spirit or ancestor.

Ancestor Call

I call to those who came before me,
Whose blood flows in my veins,
Whose body has made my bones,
Whose breath gave me life,
Whose spirit guides my own.
Come be with me here now!

Mighty Dead Call

I call to those who came before me,
Those who have walked this path ahead of me
With wisdom, strength, and grace.
I honor your memory.
Come dance with me tonight!

If you don't feel like a connection was made in the ritual, pay attention to your dreams that night. Also be on the lookout for any interesting signs moving forward, such as coins showing up in odd places, smelling the person's signature perfume, or seeing symbols from your childhood that you associate with the person.

Connecting with the Spirits of Place

The land upon which we live directly influences our practice. It is literally the foundation, the ground we build upon. What we consume from the land becomes part of our body. When we die, we return to the land. Our surroundings, our environment, our spheres of existence are our world—the natural and human-made phenomena alike. We tend to think of the Witch as being out in nature, forgetting that urban environments have their own spirit as well. The places we find ourselves in and the spaces we create both have power. The power of those places can either fuel us or deplete us, depending on how we interact with them. That is why we're addressing these energies with the Witch Bones.

Interacting with the spirits of place begins with acknowledging them. There are actually multiple layers of spirits and energies to work with in any given location. People often make the mistake of identifying the spirits of a location as being a solitary entity, but they are more like a collective, made up of many individuals that are a part of the greater form. Think of a medium- to large-size city. No matter what city you're thinking of, I guarantee it has distinctive neighborhoods, often with their own names they are best known by. The postal address may list the city name, but when you go to that area, you're likely to say you're going to "the East Side," "the Battery," or "College Hill." Each of those areas is made up of streets with their own vibes, as well as homes, businesses, and public spaces. Each of those buildings and places is unique—and they each have smaller sections within that are also distinctive. Then there are the people, plants, animals, and other beings that live in those places. That's how the spirits of place work.

That might seem overwhelming, but I find the best place to start is with and in your own home, and then work out from there—literally. I recommend that you sit on the floor in the center of the space (if you can), create your magic sphere, light a candle (mainly for mood and focus), close your eyes, breathe, and reach out into the space in your mind's eye. Start in your apartment or house and get a sense of the energy of the space.[11] It has its own spirit, largely made up of the energies of who built the space, who lived there before you, and who lives there now. Say hello and introduce yourself. Then continue to

11. If you're in a multiplex, then the next thing to do after communing with your apartment is to acknowledge the building in which you are situated. Then continue on to the land that it's on.

move outward and reach out to the immediate lot of land the building sits on. Next, move to the block that you live on, the neighborhood, and so forth. Go as far out as you feel comfortable with for your area. I tend to choose about four spots in advance that correspond to natural or human-made landmarks in my area and may also align with the cardinal directions. For example, these landmarks could be bodies of water, mountains, monuments, sculpture, bridges, parks, or forests. If these locations have special meaning for you, that tends to make the exercise a little more personal and profound.

You might even encounter some surprises along the way—entities or energies you didn't even know were there. Remember to be respectful. I also recommend physically visiting spots around your area and connecting with them on location. Consider leaving an environmentally safe offering, and don't take anything without asking permission first, even if it seems inconsequential, like a pebble, dirt, or a flower. If you're unsure what to leave as an offering, simply say, "I acknowledge and appreciate you." Taking photos is also a very non-invasive way of having a reminder of that place.

Again, this all may seem like a lot to take in, but just remember to start small and local. Get familiar with the founding spirits of where you live, little by little. It takes so little effort to be more aware of your surroundings and communicate with them. Just taking a breath and saying hello and listening for a moment is a good place to start.

Houses with Good Bones

While we're addressing the spirits of place, it's a good idea to think a little more consciously about your immediate residence and the energies that make it up. If things feel a little out of sorts, what can you do?

It is a common misconception that the first thing you should do when you move into a new place as a Witch is to cleanse the fuck out of it. Chances are, you responded positively to a place and selected it because of the good feeling it gave you. Those vibes are likely because of the existing vibrations that are already there. You are going to add your own vibrations to the mix, but that doesn't mean you need to wipe the slate clean. You don't have to give it a hard, sterile spiritual wipe-down. The same is true for when your space needs an adjustment further on down the road.

For example, I live in a house built in 1927. It's not super old compared to most of the houses in New England (Providence, Rhode Island, was founded in 1636!), but it's got some age. When my partner and I viewed the house, we both got the feeling that the house was like "a warm, embracing hug." It gave off the energy that it had been cared for, and as its new owners, we wanted to recognize the caretaker spirit within it—and let it know that we very much wanted to continue building its legacy. So while I did clean the home so we could settle in, I also did workings to introduce ourselves to the house, which has proven extremely useful.

In contrast, the house we had rented in Seattle was built around 1901, and had seen its fair share of college students and, no doubt, tumultuous relationships. While the energy of the house didn't exactly feel bad, it definitely felt unsure, uneasy, and a bit mistrustful. There was a definite caretaker spirit, but it felt like a cranky old man who was braced to deal with more trouble. I gave the house an extremely thorough physical cleansing, washing down everything from ceiling to floor. I then dispensed with the unstable spiritual entities and residue while seeking to make a truce with the old man energy (and resident ghost cats). After we were there for a while, the uneasiness lifted and a sense of appreciation settled in. However, from time to time—especially when we had been gone traveling for a while, or when things got a bit messy because we were so busy working—something weird would happen. Luckily it was always something that wasn't too severe and could be fixed pretty quickly, but there was definitely a pattern to it. But considering how the outcomes of those issues could have been a lot worse (like when the electrical box got flooded or the heater mysteriously burned out), I also feel there was a general concern for keeping the house intact and stable. It stressed us out, but in the end, the house was improved upon.

My Taurean partner, Nathan, says that he is happiest at home when (and I quote) "everything has its place." It's difficult for him to compose and create when there are boxes and piles of stuff and other clutter. That's not to say a huge mess isn't going to happen when the work is actually happening—there will be instruments and books everywhere. But in order for him to start work, to feel at ease and motivated, the space has to be in order. I'm the same way about my studio and starting new projects.

If you're going to do a cleansing ritual in your bathroom or cook a magical meal in your kitchen, you'll benefit from physically cleaning and organizing the space first. Why? Things flow better, the space feels invigorated and ready, and you're not distracted by mess. You're respecting not only your work, but also the space you're working in, as well as yourself. Whenever I come home from tour, it doesn't matter how clean the cat/house-sitter left the place—I still need to clean the house and put things away to regain a sense of order and well-being.

Putting things in order, realizing what is useful, important, and/or meaningful to you, can greatly improve pretty much everything. While house cleaning might not be a cure for everyone's ills, it can greatly reduce anxiety and depression for some people, while also giving us a sense of control over our environment—or better yet, a sense of having a greater impact upon it. This is something I can personally attest to. Putting things in order doesn't mean throwing everything away or losing your personality or the identity that you may associate with certain things. It's an opportunity to curate your collections, refresh your altar space, set up protections and wards, and try new things.

☾ WITCHUAL ☽
Rebalancing the Home

When things feel out of sorts in my home, I address our hearth altar first, even if another area of the house is generating the concerning energy. The hearth is essentially the center of our home and practice, so it sets the vibe and foundation for the rest of the home.

I make sure the altar is clean and has fresh candles and offerings, and I light some incense. Then I go about tidying other parts of the house until things feel better. Here is a little charm to think about as you do this:

> *Everything has its order and its place.*
> *Gone the unneeded that takes up space.*

Broken Bones

Our bones are strong and flexible, but they are not invincible. Whether through an accident or impact, bone is sometimes put under more stress or pressure than it can handle, causing it to break. So how does that translate for our magical bodies? Breaking magical bones can mean breaking with tradition, separating from a group, experiencing burnout, or making a mistake in your practice that trips you up.

When we break an actual bone, the procedure is to get an X-ray to see what's gone wrong, set the bone back into position, give it plenty of support with a cast, and then rest and have patience while it heals. The same advice is applicable to our magical broken bones. We must evaluate the break, determine the best course of action (mending or discarding), seek support and assistance to help us find our way, and most especially give ourselves space to heal.

While the best remedy for broken bones is time and patience, it's important not to let fear stop us from moving forward. When we've been hurt or otherwise traumatized, we may avoid trying anything again. We may be afraid to trust ourselves or anyone else. Being cautious or even wary is fine. There are lessons to be learned in breaking bones—which include knowing the warning signs so we don't have a repeat incident.

If you're feeling uncertain, remember your Witch Lungs, Heart, and Serpent. Breathe and recognize your sovereignty of self, find your rhythm and remember what moves you, and listen to your intuition and take the necessary precautions. You'll be ready to try again, but now with more wisdom and insight.

Witch Bones Sigil

Use the Witch Bones Sigil as a meditational focus for connecting with tradition and ancestral wisdom. Begin with the 3 Breaths exercise, then draw the sigil on a piece of paper. You could also choose to paint it on a bone that you have found or were given. Place the paper or bone upon your altar and light a small candle or tealight. Recite the poem at the beginning of this chapter. Then follow with the Aligning the Bodies exercise while focusing on the sigil.

Witch Bones Sigil

Chapter 5
The Weaver

The woven and the weaver are we,
Weft and warp, the whole pattern to see.
Strung through our hearts and made by our hands,
Electric pulses down ancient lands.
Liminal spaces, magical hour,
Summoning spirit, cauldron power.

Not only does a Weaver work the threads of a loom, creating a pattern as they go, but they also know the color and weight of each thread, often just by feel alone. They may have even been the one to collect the fibers, to spin them into thread, and to dye them in a cauldron. All throughout this process, the Weaver keeps a picture in mind of what they wish to create on the loom.

The Weaver is the Mind of the Witch. This Witch Mind is in charge of coalescing the information from the rest of the Witch anatomy—collecting, organizing, and disseminating every thread. It is a cauldron of creativity, the problem solver, a designer, and mission control. The Witch Mind is also the gateway and conduit for spirit.

Let us find out more about who the Weaver is, and take a peek at the electric show that happens within our nerves. Let us voyage through the stars to explore the network of the divine body, the power of memory, emotions, and our senses, and revel in the beauty of magic.

The Hierophant
The house ruled by spirit.

The Emperor gave you structure and foundation, rooted in the strength of Earth and blended with the gifts of Air, Fire, and Water. Now the fifth element emerges with the Hierophant: Spirit. The Hierophant is here to bring spiritual guidance and direction, to remind you of those metaphysical and symbolic tools that await your direction. The loom sits ready to receive its tapestry. However, you're not here to follow spiritual orders from someone else—the spirit you encounter here is yourself. The resident deity in the temple is you.

That means it's up to you to call the shots. The Hierophant card bears the number 5, which in the tarot represents learning the pros and cons of cycles: when they're healthy and when we must change them in order to break free. It's up to you as the resident deity to observe the cycles and circles found within your body. This is the domain of Spirit.

The Hierophant asks: What do you take of the traditions you have learned from your Bones, and what new ones shall you forge on the road ahead? What stars shall guide you on your journey? What fibers should you select to weave your pattern strong? Are you ready to be the one in charge?

Hey, Star Stuff

As you might have guessed, the Witch Mind is the brain of the Witch's anatomy, acting as the command and control center of the body. Just as the brain functions in our own bodies, coordinating the messages it receives, the Witch Mind collects and processes information from the other parts of the body. It guides our decisions and helps put everything in order. The Witch Mind illuminates the rest of the body and creates the larger orbit that we move in—much like the sun. It is the star that guides us.

Right now, your brain is sending signals via your nervous system to the rest of the systems in your body, which is made up of organs made of tissues made of cells. Those little cells with their even tinier organelles are doing their jobs. Those cells are made up of atoms, which are made up of subatomic particles in motion. Those same kinds of particles are also found in everything from the chair you're sitting on to the tree outside, the mountain beyond, the meteor passing by, the moons orbiting Jupiter, and the sun itself. This means that you too—yes, you—are made of star stuff.

Stepping outside of the universe of our own bodies for a moment, we can see ourselves as cells that are part of groups (families and communities), which are part of systems (cities and states), and larger bodies (countries), and so forth. An individual person may seem small, but they can still be very influential in their own way. Which means the microcosm (you) can and does affect the macrocosm (the world). You do have just as much impact on the world around you as your cells have on you, if not more. Your body is a universe that you are the deity of—your own personal starship. It's yours: you maintain and control your body and give it direction, to the best of your ability.

Magic and the Electric Chariots of Thought

When the poet Walt Whitman wrote "I Sing the Body Electric," I wonder if he had any concept of the electricity that runs through our bodies every moment we live. He did identify as a humanist, which is rooted in the philosophy that emphasizes the value and agency of human beings (both as individuals and as a collective). The poem itself praises and honors the human body and recognizes that the soul is not separate from the body but is an integral part of it. At the very end, he writes, "O I say these are not the parts and poems of the body only, but of the soul." If our parts and words make up both body and soul, then to sing them electric is to speak of the charge or vital spark within. So maybe Whitman *did* know in his own way. He definitely touched on a nerve, that's for sure.

Our nerve cells or neurons are incredible messengers working our very own information superhighway. Neurons emit and receive tiny electrical impulses throughout the body, transmitting signals and commands at the synapses. Synapses are microscopic junctions—literally the liminal gaps between the fibers of each nerve cell—where the axon terminals can pass along information to the next cell.

This fact makes me think of two amazing things. First, at the very fiber of our being is a network of threads in space. As a Witch, I see my work as weaving threads—we and everything around us are threads on a universal loom, weaving in and out through time, space, and consciousness; with visible and invisible connections and changes happening within and all around us. Second, on a much larger scale, new discoveries in space suggest that there are giant invisible structures or cosmic webs present in our galaxy that gave it mass and form.[12] Sit with that for a moment. Our bodies are neural nets; the universe is made up of cosmic webs. These threads and connections are both visible and invisible and very much real, regardless of whether we're aware of them or not.

Here's another fascinating thing: we tend to associate thought with just our brain, but what if we look at these nerve signals and impulses as thoughts from the rest of our body? Really, what is the difference (besides location) between the thoughts that originate from our conscious, subconscious, and unconscious minds and those signals from our heart, lungs, stomach, and other organs? They're all electric pulses carried by cells.

There's even medical evidence for this connection, as discovered in the recorded experiences of organ transplant recipients. Medical Daily reports that "the heart ultimately stores memories through…nerve cells.…The behaviors and emotions acquired by the recipient from the original donor are due to…memories stored in the neurons of the organ donated."[13] Patient recipients reported personality changes in "food, music, art, sexual, recreational, and career preferences in addition to name associations and sensory experiences" that were parallel to the information gathered about the donor.

If our organs are thinking and causing change in our bodies, then the thoughts that originate from our minds can impact not only ourselves but the world around us as well. We are giant neurons sending signals into liminal spaces—and receiving them as well.

12. EurekAlert! "Dark 'Noodles' May Lurk in the Milky Way," American Association for the Advancement of Science (AAAS), January 21, 2016; and Alison Klesman, "Galaxies Are Locked in Place by Their Surroundings," Astronomy, June 13, 2017. https://www.eurek alert.org/pub_releases/2016-01/ca-dm011416.php.

13. Lizette Borreli, "Can An Organ Transplant Change A Recipient's Personality? Cell Memory Theory Affirms 'Yes,'" Medical Daily, July 9, 2013. https://www.medicaldaily.com/can -organ-transplant-change-recipients-personality-cell-memory-theory-affirms-yes-247498.

Thoughts have power. This is a fundamental lesson of magic: what we think impacts ourselves and the world around us. We tend to be dismissive of thought, but consider the process and effects of thought, both intentional and unconscious. Emotion combined with thought can have powerful effects on our bodies, from the detrimental effects of stress to the rewards of joy and ecstasy. If these "non-physical" things can have a dramatic impact on our bodies, then why can't they affect the world around us? The body language of an angry person can set everyone on edge, even if the person hasn't said a word or raised a fist, in the same way that seeing someone smile from the heart can bring a smile to our own lips. Yes, these are visual clues, but they start with thought and focus. We are transmitting thought in the form of our ideas and emotions, building, weaving, and changing patterns as we live.

Making Emotions and Experiences

In recognizing the magic of thought, we can find power in our emotions as well. Society has long had a nasty habit of downplaying and dismissing emotions—especially who can have them, when, where, and why. Toxic stereotypes that demand that men shouldn't cry or show "weakness" and that women shouldn't be aggressive or strong are both highly limiting and damaging. Subjugating and relegating emotions can be physically harmful in so many ways. If we're free to feel and explore emotions, we find that our minds and bodies feel healthier.

One of my favorite podcasts is *Invisibilia* from NPR. This show explores "the invisible forces that shape human behavior—things like ideas, beliefs, assumptions and emotions." I highly recommend it if you love sorting out the mysteries of the mind like I do. On June 1, 2017, *Invisibilia* released the first of two episodes focused on emotions, which is where the work of Lisa Feldman Barrett is introduced. Barrett is a professor of psychology at Northeastern University and a researcher at Harvard Medical School and the Massachusetts General Hospital. In an NPR interview also released on the same day, she said: "Your brain is organized in such a way as to [make] anticipatory guesses about what is going to happen next. And this is happening entirely outside of your awareness. You have past experiences, and those experiences become wired into your brain, and then your brain uses those past experiences to make guesses about the immediate future. So, emotions aren't happening to you. Your brain makes them as you need them. You are the architect of your own experience. It's just that most of this is happening outside of your awareness."[14]

Our brains are constantly curating the information they receive, creating how we see the world. These filters and our responses to our experiences are a result of the programming we acquire as we grow up, built from what we learn and encounter. Barrett's theory that the brain is responsible for making our emotions is another opportunity for finding power in them. Emotions can seem scary because they make us feel out of control. But if we seek to connect more fully with ourselves and be present in our experiences, then we are no longer a bystander. As Barrett says, we become the architects. We have the power to build our experiences if we are willing to take the next step. That's not to say that any sort of emotional work is easy or fast—because it rarely is. But change is possible if we participate in the work.

Receiving Signals: Connecting with the Divine

So your organs are thinking, your neurons are messaging, and you're changing your experience through your ideas and emotions as you interact with the cosmic web. But who's really in the control tower? A soul? A god? A spirit? It's time to meet the divine aspect of yourself.

You *can* practice Witchcraft without ever involving gods and goddesses. But I would argue that it's a lot harder to effectively walk this path without at least acknowledging the spirit that dwells within you. Once you recognize the self-divine as yourself, it becomes a lot easier to recognize it in the world around you—including other people, animals, plants, places, and beyond. The self-divine is the final key to unlocking the chains that have kept you disconnected from the world and yourself.

Envision yourself as a thread. Your body contains one end of the thread and the rest of it flows up out of your head far beyond you. The rest connects

---

14. Lisa Feldman Barrett, "The Making of Emotions, from Pleasurable Fear to Bittersweet Relief," interview by Rebecca Hersher, NPR, June 1, 2017. https://www.npr.org/sections /health-shots/2017/06/01/530103479/the-making-of-emotions-from-pleasurable-fear-to -bittersweet-relief.

to the universal loom or cosmic web. But the thread is not just a thread—it is a connection to a larger part of our own spirit. Whether it joins up with a god-ball of divine yarn, a hall of ancestors, or a giant computer, it's a means of both sending and receiving information. You are an active part of the process, fully integrated. You truly are the weaver and the web, all at once.

It might seem weird or even heretical to see yourself as a god or recognize that divinity is present in you. You might be comfortable with the idea of multiple gods but still hesitant to believe in your own divine nature. It's hard to overcome a lifetime of indoctrination. Yet myths are littered with the idea that gods and other divine beings do visit us from time to time. I would argue that saints, saviors, demigods, and prophets point more to the evidence that the divine is right here. Perhaps this physical existence is just one branch of a giant strand of DNA, but you're still part of the spiral structure that holds it all together.

If you are able to recognize the divine within, it can in turn improve your relationship with deities and other spiritual beings. You will see them mirrored in yourself and vice versa. Recognition dispels unhealthy myths and allows you to grow in new ways. This is why it's so important for folks to be able to see images of divinity that reflect their own gender, skin color, sexuality, and other defining characteristics. Representation matters because it allows you to find the divine within.

Divinity isn't about achieving or existing as perfection. Perfection is a static and small-minded concept that is foreign in an ever-evolving and shifting universe. Nor is divinity about being all-knowing or all-powerful or having extraordinary powers. You being a spirit present in a body, though, is an amazing thing worthy of revel. The world is full of wonder and magic, and you have an active role if you choose to participate. Divinity is found in being present and ever-changing, qualities found within the anatomy of the Witch—yet another reminder that you do indeed belong here.

Be the Weaver

With your bodies aligned, your ability to engage with your magic is drastically enhanced. There are just a few things that can act as stumbling blocks because there's a lot of confusion out there regarding how magic works, what you need to do it, and how to do it ethically. All of that mess can make you hesitate about taking hold of your own threads and affirming your place as the Weaver of your existence.

I think most people do want to believe in magic, but have been told for so long that magic isn't real, that it's all fantasy, that they're weird, a freak, or delusional for even considering it. Who benefits from you not feeling like you can affect the world around you? Who can control you when you give your power to someone else? Think about it. Consider the crossroads of art, science, and magic that we've explored up to this point, and give yourself the freedom to own your power. Believe in your anatomy as a Witch.

A lot of people say they believe in magic, but then they dismiss their own magical power, believing it exists in other things and beings rather than in themselves. You can gather all of the stuff, but if you don't believe in magic, you're less likely to see the results you want. A broken clock is right twice a day, but if it's not wound, it's not really working to its full capacity. Basically, the stuff can make it *look* right, but it's up to you to make magic work. Don't get me wrong—stuff can absolutely have power, without a doubt. But when you take the time to understand why and how these external components work, the change is much more significant. Consider why you would choose any plant, color, aroma, mineral, or solar or lunar date over another one. What is the meaning and significance of these elements and alignments? Furthermore, consider the source—be it the folklore of the spell you're using, or where the plant grew, or where the rock originated. The more actively involved you are in the process, the more you enhance your connection and understanding. Essentially, be sure you know why you choose certain components, how they work, and where they came from. This is especially helpful when you have limited resources and therefore know why you can make do with the most simplest and accessible of things—and get the same results.

The last hurdle is tackling responsibility, morals, and ethics. Humanity has made so many rules and doctrines throughout history. Many of them were designed with the intent to help make society safer and healthier. However, in many cases, determining who benefits from those rules can certainly be a point of argument, depending on who gets restricted or punished. You must consider who holds the power and whose vision are you actually following.

When it comes to magic, there are natural laws and human rules. "Magic follows the path of least resistance" is a natural law that you can observe repeatedly. People love imposing the human rules on others though, usually without fully understanding what they're talking about. You don't have to go far online to see people quoting "the Rede" as a reason why you shouldn't do certain kinds of magic. Little do they realize that "the Rede" is part of a much older and larger collection of folklore that is meant to be an aid, not a set of restrictions.

The "threefold law of return," or "rule of three," that gets attributed to the Wiccan Rede is one of those human rules that was not so elegantly derived from natural law. We find mention of the threefold law in Gwen Thompson's collected *Rede of the Wiccae*: "Mind the Threefold Law ye should / Three times bad an' three times good."[15] We see variations of the concept appear in *Buckland's Complete Book of Witchcraft*, published in 1986, where he discusses karma, threefold retribution, and return.[16] About the same time, Amber K introduced an eight-line long version of the Rede, altering the verse to "And ever mind the Rule of Three: What ye send out, comes back to thee," which she later published in *True Magick* in 1990.

But going back to Gwen's version, it's fascinating to note that the lore surrounding the Rede never describes what the "threefold law" is or mentions anything about "return." There are several other threefold descriptions in the collected lore of that tradition, but they are connected to divinity and other revelations and most especially to esoteric notions of the mind, body, and soul.

Concerning the Witch Mind (and the rest of the magical body), I find this extremely relevant to looking at magic in a revolutionary way that is far more helpful to magical practitioners. I don't think the threefold law as it was originally mentioned in Gwen's Rede has anything to do with retribution or punishment.

15. Robert Mathiesen and Theitic, *The Rede of the Wiccae* (Providence, RI: Olympian Press, 2005), 53.

16. Raymond Buckland, *Buckland's Complete Book of Witchcraft* (St. Paul, MN: Llewellyn, 1986), 86.

Instead you should look at doing magic in terms of how it affects you physically, mentally, and spiritually—*that* threefold. When you do magic, you should be taking into consideration how it can affect your body, mind, and spirit, for better or for worse. In turn, your actions have real-world effects, some positive, some negative—good and bad being a matter of perspective.

You can also integrate another threefold concept into your magical practice: past, present, and future. This view comes in handy to avoid continuously doing what I call "magical triage." Magical triage is running from one problem or crisis to the next, treating the symptoms rather than identifying the root cause of the problem. If you can step back to examine a problem—see what led up to it (the past), consider immediate solutions (the present), and chart a course to eliminate the problem going forward (the future)—your workings become far more effective.

Here is an example of magical triage versus a more rooted working. Let's say you are short on funds to pay bills. You do a quick money spell and a hundred dollars comes your way. Great, that solves the cash-flow problem temporarily—but you have a feeling you'll be dealing with this same problem again next month. The real reason you're short on funds is because your job isn't paying you enough or maybe isn't providing benefits that would offset your living expenses/medical bills. You could do a working that brings you a better job or helps you negotiate for a raise and better benefits in your current position. That would make a more significant change in your life presently and in the foreseeable future.

Changing your approach to how you work magic can open up greater possibilities. It's a bit like working with only two colors of thread because you didn't know there were other options—and then finding the thread cabinet that has ALL of the colors. There may be greater responsibility with having more choices, but you also will have more opportunities. You'll increase your perception and strengthen your metaphysical design skills. The more you exercise the Weaver, the better your Witchcraft becomes.

Sensational Details

Consider this rhyme, also from *The Rede of the Wiccae*: "Soft of eye an' light of touch / Speak little, listen much."[17] Chock full of the senses, these few words possess a lot of wisdom worth contemplating. "Soft of eye" can mean shifting your vision to look at the world differently, but also not jumping to conclusions about something you may see. To be "light of touch" means having a gentle yet firm approach in what you do, so you can be both receptive to changes and take note of others' sensitivities. "Speak little, listen much" allows you to observe more of the world while having a more precise impact when you do decide to be heard.

Far too often, we can get so caught up in our minds that we fail to take proper notice of the world around us. Most of the secrets of the Witch are uncovered simply through observation—by paying attention to the patterns around us. That includes the patterns happening in our own bodies, which tend to be the ones we overlook the most. Yet how we experience the world is so dependent on how we see, feel, taste, and smell the world around us. If we miss those crucial clues—the ones staring back at us in the mirror every day—what else are we missing?

It may seem obvious to say, "See with your eyes and listen with your ears," but few people really pay attention to what they are seeing or listening to, especially if they're focused on what to say next, instead of listening to what the other person is saying right now. The best conversations develop slowly and grow with exploration, versus those when we're focused on trying to maintain social niceties/expectations. It's a hard habit to break, because we often want to be recognized for what we are saying at the expense of someone else who wants exactly the same.

Our eyes are the sense most likely to mislead us, especially if we're going on just a glance or a movement. A peek into other realms and otherworldly beings often doesn't happen when you're looking straight at something, but rather is something glimpsed or tracked in the periphery. Looking straight at

---

17. Mathiesen and Theitic, *The Rede of the Wiccae*, 52.

the phenomenon is more likely to make it vanish. So instead we must soften our gaze and allow our inner vision and other senses to take over.

I feel like half of what people may attribute to being psychic is simply paying attention to the details and patterns that are right in front of you. It's so easy to get wrapped up in our phones, get distracted by ads and media or maybe what someone else said, and then miss the wealth of clues right in front of you.

What Is Nature Doing?

Regardless of whether you live out in the wilds, in suburbia, or in the heart of a city, make note of the sky, temperature, and other aspects of the weather, consider what the air smells like, and see what the plants, animals, and insects are up to. Take it another step further and see how this makes your own body feel. Changes in barometric pressure can cause headaches, humidity can make you feel weighed down, and an impending storm might make you feel anxious or excited.

What Are the People Doing?

Without being a social nuisance (no one likes being stared at), I like to observe what people around me are doing. What are they wearing? What does their body language say? What kind of mood do they seem to be in? Compare this information with any other feelings you might be getting, brought to you by your other senses. If something seems out of the ordinary, what is giving you that sensation?

When interacting directly with people as I go about my day, I try to make eye contact while connecting if it seems appropriate, safe, and permissible. Taking a moment to greet the barista instead of barking your coffee order at them might irk the person behind you, but it says to the human in front of you that you appreciate them and recognize them as a person. I know as an introvert who battles social anxiety, it can seem scary to talk to people, but it's a good exercise in building resilience.

There's a reason collecting details is called "paying attention"—you are definitely spending some time and effort doing this. But the neat thing is that the more you train your mind and body to notice those details, the more automatic it becomes. You'll start to realize that you're retaining more information than before, making connections more quickly, and even predicting outcomes or solutions well ahead of everyone else.

Sigil to Enhance Psychic Vision

This sigil won't exactly give you psychic superpowers. Rather, what it will do is help your Witch Mind recognize that you are seeking to enhance and build upon what's already in your wheelhouse. Working with this sigil signifies a dedication to pay greater attention to those little details. To become familiar with this sigil, draw it on a purple or dark blue candle at the new moon. Place some anointing oil on your fingertip and touch the carved sigil on the candle, then touch the finger to your temple/third eye and say:

> *By the dark of moon and coming light,*
> *I do seek the path that grants clear sight.*
> *Knowledge and wisdom, vision be clear,*
> *So that I may weave threads far and near.*
> *May my spirit within guide me true,*
> *Open my eyes to the hidden view.*

If you wish to ask any specific spirits, deities, or ancestors to help you, add your own couplet to the end of the charm to properly address them. Here is an example:

> *Great-Grandmom Sarah, I call to you.*
> *Come be by my side this journey through.*

Sigil to Enhance Psychic Vision

Listening to the Silence

I remember when I was little saying to someone, "Can you hear the silence too?" That sounded weird even to me as soon as I said it, and I'm sure they just brushed it off as kid-speak. Maybe they said, "Yes, it's a quiet day," in reply. But I didn't mean that it was quiet or that there was literally no sound. I was referring to a sensation I was perceiving through my ears. It was a beautiful spring day, and in our breezeway, the world felt content and at ease. It sounded (without being an audible sound) like a soft, continuous hum or breath, but it wasn't made by bees, the wind, or leaves whispering. As I've grown older, I've been in all sorts of places—indoors and outside—that generate that same sense of silence. I attribute it to a collective spiritual state of a place.

I've found that other Witches pick up this resonant silence as well, or at least experience it in similar ways. You might too. Have you ever heard someone say, "I didn't like the feeling of that room" or "This place has such a good feel to it"? They're not talking about the interior decorating. While visual elements can certainly create a visceral response—such as a stark white examining room that reads as sterile and cold, or an incredibly messy room that feels disorienting—there's often an underlying feeling that may influence the activities you're responding to on the surface. That feeling likely has its roots in human or spirit activities that happened previously (either recently or spanning centuries, depending on what occurred) and have left a psychic impression in that place.

Walk into a room and situate yourself comfortably in the center of it (seated or standing, it doesn't matter). Close your eyes. In your mind's eye, visualize the room around you as it is right now. Where is the doorway? How many windows are there? What is the floor surface made of? What furniture and notable objects are in it? Next listen to the room itself. Can you hear anything? Is that the radiator or air conditioner making noise—and can you sense where it is coming from? Can you hear anything coming from outside or from another room? Is there a dog snoring in the room? Is there anything making you feel uneasy in the room, or do you feel comfortable and safe?

Sometimes you can even summon that silence if you focus on it, almost like pulling up a recording on a device or shutting off extra noise until you can hear just that one level of sound. I find it can be used for meditation as well as attuning with a space.

Tackling Aphantasia

Some people don't have what is generally referred to as the mind's eye. This condition where they are unable to visualize mental images is known as *aphantasia*. Their brains process information in other ways.

With this in mind, I recognize that some readers may be frustrated with visualization exercises. There are definitely other ways of experiencing those practices that are just as effective. Processing things differently from other people does not make your magic any less effective. I think it's vital to understand that every person is unique and there are many ways to see/hear/feel the world. The key is to work to your strengths and find connections that work for you.

As a visual artist, imagery is obviously my happy place. I tend to have a delay with auditory processing, so someone telling me directions is far less successful than showing me a map or pointing out landmarks. My partner has an extremely hard time visualizing, but if I provide an image or set of descriptive words, he's able to create music by accessing musical theory and emotional quality. He's also able to tell amazing stories through song and map adventures for role-playing games. So clearly there are multiple ways to utilize imagination and engage with our minds.

Meditation, visualization, trance—these are all similar altered states of the mind. Everyone can experience trance; it's part of how our brains work. The problem is that we have a lot of negative or seemingly boring ways of describing different states of trance: daydreaming, spacing out, losing track, being in the groove, getting absorbed in something.

Furthermore, especially in magical communities, we tend to connect trance states with extraordinary things, as well as the need for using substances to achieve those divine experiences. Far too often I hear someone lamenting that maybe they just don't have the right magical skills because they're not having these Hollywood movie special-effects experiences. But if you sit down and talk with them for a bit, they indeed have had remarkable experiences—they simply didn't recognize them as such, because they didn't fit their expectation or sound like what that other Witch or magician described. Or the circumstances didn't seem particularly special—for example, sitting at their desk versus being naked dancing around a bonfire slathered in sweat and herbal grease. It all comes down to building a practice and allowing for awareness.

Trance is the result of being in sync with the universe and out of sync with the perceived or expected social paradigm. It is all part of the same universe—we're all made from the same star stuff. What's different is how we relate to and process the world around us. Sometimes all you have to do is walk one more step out of your regular routine and look at the normal a little out of focus, and suddenly you see things differently. The barrier is largely the space between expectation and actuality. I think far too many people discount their own abilities and the power they have to manifest magic in the world around them. If you look at the ordinary long enough, you can start to see the spaces in between, and without expectation, you can indeed experience the extraordinary.

Regardless of how your neural pathways are knitted, you are the Weaver of your own path and pattern. How you see the world is unique to your experience—it can't and won't match up exactly to anyone else's. That means how and what you weave is totally up to you, as is your working style. You get to choose the stars that make up the constellation of you.

Sigil of the Weaver

Use the Sigil of the Weaver as a meditational focus for helping you align your Witch Mind. Light a candle and focus on it as you perform the 3 Breaths. Recite the poem at the beginning of this chapter. Sit in complete silence for three minutes and allow yourself to simply listen and be. Pay close attention to any dreams you may have immediately following this meditation.

Sigil of the Weaver

Chapter 6

Loving the Magical Body

O temple of breath, blood, flesh and bone,
House of my spirit, a serpent sown.
Labyrinth of being, open the door,
Following footsteps of those before.
Painted walls, candles lit, altar dressed,
My body a map of journey blessed.

Loving your own body is not always easy, especially when it causes you pain or malfunctions. The first draft of this book was written while trying to navigate the worst migraine I'd had in a very long time.[18] The irony is not lost on me that my own body was being problematic as I worked to write a book about the magical body. Nonetheless, I persisted.

But honestly, love isn't all flowers, hearts, and happily-ever-after endings. It involves actively working through challenges to create a better relationship. And you are absolutely in a relationship with your body. There are good days and bad days. As with any relationship, there needs to be regular maintenance done and attention paid to keep things healthy and functioning, not only physically but emotionally and mentally as well.

---

18. Much of that first draft met the delete key. My thanks to my editing team who managed to read that draft and kindly did not hex me for submitting it to them. Also, the second draft was worked on during the beginning of the COVID-19 pandemic.

The sacred temple always needs work. Visitors must be cleaned up after. Not everyone will appreciate you or respect your space. Some people take and others will leave offerings. But only you get to decide what the temple looks like—how you adorn, celebrate, and honor it. You can choose your opening hours and restrictions and set guidelines. You are the builder, custodian, and resident deity. Taking care of yourself is an act of love and devotion.

The Lovers

Radical self-love is a right and a ritual.

The Hierophant gives you rules, but the thing about rules is that they are made to be broken. Every taboo we as humans have placed on ourselves—we always find a way around them somehow. There are many rules about both love and bodies in particular. You must sort out where the truth lies for you. The Lovers is about learning to respect and understand yourself, to set your own rules and values. You're ready to journey forward with a renewed sense of self.

The lesson of the 5 cards in the tarot is learning to break cycles that are unhealthy for you, and learn to master those that basically gives you wheels (the freedom to move!) when you arrive at the next card in the suit, the realm of 6. The sixes focus on journeys, reunions, harmony, and the bestowing of blessings. They also recommend exercising patience, honoring what you have, being practical, planning ahead, and maintaining standards. These are all acts of love.

The Lovers embody harmony, love, attraction, and union. Two serpents, the physical and the metaphysical, are becoming intertwined like we see in the caduceus—creating a new sense of healthy balance. Rather than separating everything into vice or virtue, sacred or profane, you can choose falling in love with your magical physical body. You can experience the harmony, synergy, and union of your inner and outer lives being interwoven. By celebrating the joys of life, you can awaken new passions and reunite your multiple bodies.

Our modern culture is rooted in telling you that you have no power, that magic is silly, that you need approval from others. These ideas are unhealthy— flawed laws to be challenged. It is an act of revolution to believe in yourself. To believe in the power and beauty of your own body is a riot and an act of radical self-love.

Let us find the balance between our symbolic bodies and our earthly ones. In that liminal space, we find love where sky and earth do meet.

Reconnecting the Body

Early humanity understood that the body was sacred, integral to our existence and a conduit to the spiritual. But as time passed and civilizations rose and fell and rose again, we started to become separated from our bodies. This separation caused religious movements to condemn the body as being unsatisfactory and spiritually unclean. We sought to rise above the body, elevating the mind and distancing ourselves from the spirit.

As we reveled in our intellect, philosophers began to elevate and separate humankind from the world around us. But we are absolutely part of this amazing physical world, not above or distinct from it. Physical existence is not a punishment or something we're meant to suffer through. Far too many religions say we should focus solely on the spiritual next life, eschewing the world around us and dismissing our own embodied divinity. But we are designed to *live*!

Consider the so-called seven deadly sins: lust, gluttony, sloth, greed, wrath, pride, and envy. In the best of intentions and theories, they speak to practicing moderation, which is a wise thing. But lust, gluttony, pride, and sloth especially have long been used to vilify bodies and beings who refuse to conform to society, often going past a place of temperance and directly into extreme restriction. Consider the flawed cultural norm that it's considered natural for men to experiment sexually with multiple partners, but if a woman does the same, she's labeled a slut. The reality is that sexual exploration is healthy for any person interested, as long as it's done safely and consensually when that person is ready. Eating is a natural part of living and our society revels in glorifying the culinary arts, yet at the same time it sells diet plans, denies access to natural and healthy foods to low-income people (consider inner-city food deserts), and vilifies people of all sizes for simply being the way they are. The beauty industry is a multimillion-dollar affair, often making use of dangerous chemicals and plenty of Photoshop in its ads, yet there's the stigma that if you use makeup you're somehow fake or too vain. Sleep is essential to us both physically and mentally, but we're rewarded to sacrifice it for work and other demands—and taking time for yourself is considered selfish and lazy. You're damned if you do, damned if you don't.

But this is Witchcraft. There is no use for damnation and shame. Plain and simple: it is unhealthy to exist in this world while simultaneously looking down upon it. The planet suffers as we suffer because we as a society have largely lost or forgotten our ability to connect with the land, animals, plants, and other beings. We become imprisoned in our bodies rather than being able to revel in the experience of living.

If we can learn to love and honor our bodies as they are, if we seek to embrace the body of the Witch, we can reconnect with the magic of ourselves and the world we live in. We are reminded that our bodies are our most powerful and accessible tools. Our daily rituals become acts of devotion to our own temples as well as the world around us. We can learn and reincorporate the magic our ancestors knew:

> The body's own potency turns the dance into a sacrament. In early history the body as a whole, as well as each separate aspect, was sacred. Food, drink, breath and copulation were regarded as sacred channels for the power to enter man.[19]

◎ JOURNAL PROMPT ◎
Body Count

What unhealthy ideas do you hold about your body? What are three things about your body that you appreciate?

A Body of Magic

The body and magic have a long history dating back to the earliest days of our species. This connection is quite prevalent throughout mythology and is the foundation for much of folkloric spellcraft.

---

19. Wosien, *Sacred Dance*, 20–21.

The body plays an important role in countless myths concerning deities. Greek mythology has many examples of the magical body, from Zeus birthing Athena from his forehead to Dionysus being restored back to life solely from his rescued heart and Persephone eating six pomegranate seeds, cementing her position as Queen of the Underworld. In Egyptian mythology, Isis reassembles her husband Osiris's body and brings him back to life after his brother Set murders and dismembers him. (She finds everything but his penis.) In Hindu mythology, Parvati's son Ganesha gets his elephant head after Shiva decapitates him (somewhat by accident). In Norse mythology, Odin loses one of his eyes in order to gain the wisdom of the runes. All across the planet, we find creation myths that involve building this world out of the body of chthonic or primordial deities. All of this brings to mind the saying "we are made in the image of the gods," but the opposite is also very true when you think about it: "the gods are made in our image."

As for spellcraft, anthropologists and archaeologists are continually uncovering ancient spells rooted in sympathetic magic. Sympathetic magic is one of the oldest forms of spellcraft there is. This kind of magic functions along the theories that "like attracts like," "the part affects the whole by relation," and "changes in the microcosm affect the macrocosm." We make charms of certain body parts and from certain fluids because there is the common belief that like affects like. Our minds love to find patterns and similarities, so of course when it comes to the metaphysical, we use what we know.

A simple internet search will turn up any number of recent articles concerning witch bottles that are hundreds of years old hidden in old houses and buried at sacred sites. The contents of these bottles often contain bodily fluids such as urine and blood, as well as hair, nail clippings, and other organic materials. All over the world you will find fertility charms, offerings made in the shapes of breasts, labia, uteri, and phalluses. As part of their death and afterlife rituals, the ancient Egyptians used canopic jars to preserve the stomach, intensives, lungs, and liver—while the heart remained in the body.

Nor are these practices relegated only to the past. Travel anywhere in the Mediterranean and you're likely to come across the unmistakable gaze of the "evil eye," as well as amulets in the form of hands, varying from the hamsa

(Hand of Fatima) to the mano figa and mano cornuta. In Mexico, the practice of milagros involves charms that focus on a certain area of the body as a form of magical petitioning. We continually turn to the body for inspiration because we know intuitively there's a connection to magic and power through it.

Consider the fact that our internal organs are technically occult by their very nature—they are meant to be hidden from the outside world. These organs concern themselves with the inner workings of our temple, and definitely tend to hold a secret or two, even to modern science. Many of the internal processes also affect what happens on the outside of our bodies. Working back from symptoms we may see or experience, we often have to dive deeper to determine the cause. When we think about that, it's really no mystery why our ancestors focused on different parts of the body to gain influence over ourselves and others.

While we are certainly more than the sum of our parts, we can learn to love our bodies more if we seek to find magic in our assembled parts and bodily processes. Think back to the list you made in the previous exercise. Take a little more time to consider why you like and dislike certain parts of yourself. What magical properties might you assign to each and why?

Temple Time

Temples are places of real work. Welcome to your full-time employment as temple custodian and deity. The pay's not great, but there are some awesome benefits.

Being comfortable in your own skin starts with honoring your temple. You are responsible for the upkeep, but you also get to decide how it will be adorned, what rituals maintain it, and who can worship at your altar and how. Every day you choose how you will dress, what jewelry and makeup you may apply, what you will do with your hair, and other ways to physically sustain your spirit. It may seem like a lot of work, but it is a worthwhile experience. Your temple is yours.

Remember, the body is the place where your spirit resides. I like to refer to the body as temple for the mere fact that people tend to respect sacred places like temples, churches, and shrines. If you are able to recognize the divine in those places, then you ought to recognize the divine that resides within. There-fore it becomes easier to honor and respect your body in all of its phases.

Temples tend to be complex and multi-layered. They're often designed to be visually impressive from the outside—giving a hint at what splendors are inside. The temple beckons the curious further inside to communal places that create atmosphere while hinting at mysteries. There may be writing on the walls, beautiful murals and tapestries, or stained glass windows describing the story of the god inside. One may go deeper inside the temple if permitted to visit more intimately with the residing spirit. Every temple also has restricted and secret places that only the initiated may visit.

There are a great many activities that happen at any temple. There are rituals, offerings, moments of rest, and times of extreme activity. Temples are prepared, adorned, blessed, cleaned, repaired, and maintained on a regular basis. Think about all of the ways you clean, dress, and adorn your body. We've talked a lot already about the internal and symbolic processes that aid us, but interacting with the physical absolutely enhances the experience. Your inter-actions with the tactile and visual continue to make the journey more real to you, even when you're having a hard time grasping the invisible and metaphys-ical. Ritual that engages your body helps you make these connections.

Outer Layers

The exocrine system of the body, also known as the integumentary system, is made up of our skin, hair, nails, sweat, and other related glands. Our skin is our first means of defense against germs and other dangers. It encapsulates, contains, maintains, and protects us. Our skin expands with us as we grow and defines our borders. Through it, we experience the world—touching and feel-ing as we go. It flexes and bends with our movements yet resists harm.

Emerging from our skin, our hair and nails complete the package. Though they are also a means of flexible protection, we tend to think of them as acces-sories—things that adorn our bodies naturally (for better or for worse). It's fas-cinating to consider how much of our identity is sourced from the outermost layer of us. The color and condition of our skin as it stretches across our mus-cles, bones, and fat; how we style, keep, or remove the hair on our bodies; how our nails are done (or not done)—all of these things tend to be the basis of other people's opinions about us long before we say or do a thing. There is so much social baggage wrapped up in how we look. We often feel pressured to conform and fit in. Unrealistic standards and trends can make us feel uncomfortable about our skin, weight, age, shape, hair, height, and abilities. Efforts we may take to express what we feel is our true self might be scorned, made fun of, or ruled out.

Unfortunately, there is no magic wand I can wave to make all the pain you may have suffered because of other people's close-mindedness vanish, or stop people from making ill-conceived judgments about you in the future. There's no easy way to dismantle harmful stereotypes or unhealthy and unfair standards all at once. I really wish I could, for all of us. But for just a little while here, I want you to focus on *you* finding a home in your own skin and honoring it—without the outside world's views creeping in. We both know that all of that negativity is waiting outside, but perhaps what we cover here will be a balm for your spirit and armor for your soul.

Sigil for Healing Body Image Issues

This sigil is designed to help free you from the ills of confining conformity and the harm it does to our minds and bodies. It is meant to empower you to find beauty in who you are, how you look, and most especially how you see yourself in the world. May it stimulate healing and inspire newfound love from the inside out.

To use, draw the sigil with a dry-erase marker on the mirror that you look in most often, placing it on the periphery. You could also draw it on your body with an anointing oil or makeup pen/pencil. Another option is to carve it on a white, pink, or light blue candle to work with on your altar. When you wish to focus more on releasing unhealthy ideas, burn the candle from the full moon to the new moon. When you wish to draw more love and appreciation, burn it from the new moon to the full moon.

Sigil for Healing Body Image Issues

Grow Your Own Magical Components

Unlike most other mammals, we lack a full furry covering, but our hair does help to protect us, regulate our body temperature, and extend our senses. Human beings have developed a strange mythology around hair: who can grow it, where it can grow, and at what length, color, and style. Every culture has its set of standards and taboos about the hair on our heads and the rest of our bodies too.

We have myths and fairy tales about power being contained in long hair —the stories of Samson and Rapunzel come to mind. There is a story going around online about Native American men who were enlisted in the army for the Vietnam War because of their amazing tracking abilities. They apparently lost those senses when their hair was cut to comply with army regulations. There may be some truth to that, as when we get excited or scared, the hair on the back of our neck may rise, or we may get goose bumps down our arms and legs. It's fascinating to think about.

People seeking to make changes in their lives often start with cutting and/ or dyeing their hair. Why is that? Our hair is an easy thing to have control over, the change is relatively painless, and we can quickly see the results. There is the sense that if we can change the way we look, we will also change the way we feel inside. The visual alteration can also empower us to make the bigger steps we need to take to obtain the change we desire. Our hair provides a possible gateway to the being we wish to bring forth from inside of us.

Hair isn't the only thing we can alter. Each of our fingers and toes ends in a nail. Nails are a form of protection, but they also make great tools. As an artist, my nails are constantly put to use and abuse.

Having manicured nails can be a strong statement of identity and preference, especially if your choices are considered to go against social standards. (I definitely admire the folks who can have beautiful manicures, and I've been told that all I need to do in order to have them is just not use my nails. It's an interesting thought, but no matter how careful I am, I seem cursed to mess up at least one nail after painting them while doing something as delicately as possible.) There's a multitude of options for fake nails, but anybody can simply get some nail polish and change the color on their natural nails too. It's relatively easy and inexpensive—accessible to anyone who can keep a steady hand and stand the smell. A little change in color can make a big difference!

There are a multitude of magical uses for hair and nails, as they have long been popular components in spellcraft. Strands of hair and nail clippings function strongly in the realm of sympathetic magic, especially with the belief that the part can affect the whole. Because they are both relatively abundant and easy to acquire, they are popular ingredients for any sort of magic designed to influence someone—for better or for worse. I will admit to being a tad superstitious about how I dispose of my hair and nail clippings when I'm away from home!

There is also the idea of *memento mori*, objects that remind us of death and may involve a remnant of someone who has passed on. For example, the Edwardians and Victorians made beautiful and ornate jewelry and art out of a deceased one's hair. Less morbid and more life-focused, there are traditions of locks of hair exchanged between friends or lovers to enhance their bond. Beads, threads, and braids have long been woven into hair for magical purposes as well—to protect, enhance fertility, draw love, and more.

What all of these things have in common is that they are pieces of you that can magically represent you. Either on their own separated from you or while they are still physically connected to you, they can be an influence on your body.

◎ JOURNAL PROMPT ◎
Very Superstitious?

No matter where on Earth or when in history you look, you'll find magical connections centering on our hair and nails. Think about your associations with your own hair and nails. What do you believe is acceptable or prohibited? Where did those ideas come from? Do you have any superstitions about them?

Adorning the Temple

While there are some things that are difficult or impossible to change about our bodies, we can choose how we adorn them. Cosmetics, body art, clothing, and jewelry can all help us to transform and empower our bodies. They project a sense of identity that we can feel internally.

Magical Makeup

Makeup is an easy and accessible way to express ourselves. The use of cosmetics goes back to ancient times when we used both mineral and plant pigments to stain our skin and hair—such as ochre, henna, and indigo. The Egyptians used kohl (made of antimony sulfide) to darkly line their eyes, and numerous berries have been used all over the world to stain lips and cheeks. Whether makeup is used to accent the body to attract, to enhance or establish identity, or to aid in spiritual transformation, there is power involved.

Glamour may seem like illusion, but it's also a way to bring out our inner personality. What we see enhances and enforces what we may feel about ourselves on the inside. Think of it as bringing the inside to the outside, versus parroting the tired old line "beauty is only skin deep." This idiom declares that physical attractiveness does not guarantee real substance or character. While that may be handy to keep in mind, if you use all of your senses as a Witch, you're more likely to get a more holistic view of any person you encounter, regardless of what they look like. If you're paying attention, then many (if not all) of the clues are there, regardless of what may seem to be in front you. People who claim that makeup is trickery or fake tend to also be those who were judging only the surface in the first place.

Makeup can also help us explore other possibilities. It is one of the simplest forms of shapeshifting outside of costuming and attire. As children we are experts in make-believe and often love to play dress-up. As adults, we may delight in cosplay and masquerade balls, because they harken back to that sense of play and the possibility of being anything we wish. With makeup, we can see ourselves transformed before our very eyes, and that excites our spirit.

☾ WITCHUAL ☽
Makeup Charm

Applying makeup can definitely be a ritual unto itself, especially if you think about why you're putting it on and how it makes you feel. Even if it's just for you, think about what effect are you looking to achieve, and if you're going out into the world, what do you wish others to see? From setup to physical preparation to the actual application, you can find magic in the process. There can even be a magical way of thinking for when you remove the makeup.

Makeup Charm

Painted lip, eyes so bright
Shadow, brush, beauty sight
Skin and soul, glamour art
What I wish makes the part!

The Illustrated Skin

Tattooing is an ancient practice found all over the world. These skin-deep marks have been used to adorn, beautify, protect, define, and identify. There are also taboos forbidding tattoos, as well as cultural stigmas of all kinds. When we mark our skin, we are illustrating part of our life story and experiences. For some people, tattoos commemorate important life events or display for the world what we love and hold dear. For others they are marks of devotion, honoring a deity, saint, or deceased loved one. They can mark new beginnings, commitments, or even endings.

At the time of this writing, I have seven tattoos (eight, if you count the black line on my middle finger where I sliced it with an inked copper plate in college), and I'm sure there will be more. The first is the face of Kali Ma (or Durga, depending on the company) on my upper back—for protection and as a mark of devotion. Then I designed a sleeve featuring the silent film star Theda Bara, surrounded by roses and peacock feathers (both personal symbols) for my left arm. For my next piece I worked with a mentor to design a seal of heart-based guidance and protection that was placed over my sternum. Then I designed two sigils for the fronts of my thighs to help balance my mind and my path. Next was a snake that curls around my left wrist, incorporating the lunar cycle and a symbol for Baba Yaga. The most recent piece, situated just up my forearm, is also related to Baba Yaga. It's one of my drawings depicting her mobile hut dancing on chicken legs. One of my dear friends and former dance student Samara got a smaller matching version of the same design on her foot. I can look at my skin and see my life's journey in motion.

If you choose to get tattooed, the best advice I can give you is take the time to find an artist whose portfolio of work resonates with you. Don't go on price or availability alone—the time and money of work done by a solid artist is worth the effort. There are many artists working today who incorporate magic and ritual into their process, so that can be an added bonus if you can find one.

Otherwise, you can make it a ritual experience on your own. Keeping pre-appointment instructions in mind, you can perform a ritual bath or cleansing to prepare your mind and body. You can set up sacred space either mentally or physically (by walking) around the chair where the work will be done, calling in the elements and any spirits/deities to aid in the process. During the process, focus your breathing to attune with the intention of the work. Afterward, be mindful as you apply the healing ointment (as instructed) and tend to the area. By following this procedure with all of my ink, I've experienced faster healing times with no complications and have been thrilled with the end results.

Second Skins and Shiny Things

I would be remiss to not touch upon the layers of adornment we layer on top of our skin in the form of clothing and jewelry. Whether we wear clothes to conform to social ideas of modesty and propriety, use them as vehicles for aesthetic exploration, or simply see them as a means of protection from the weather, we are bringing another layer of identity to our bodies.

Just like tattoos and makeup, my clothing is often an extension of my personality. My goal is to be as me as possible, suiting my mood and goals of the day. I choose attire that makes me feel good, confident, and ready to get work done, though I will admit that this quote from the movie *Sister Act* tends to snipe out at me, because subtle is not my strong suit: "That is not a person you can hide. That is a conspicuous person designed to stick out." Then again, why would I be hiding who I am?

Think about what's in your closet. I bet you have clothes for work, clothes for relaxing, clothes for certain activities, and clothes for special occasions. You might even have garments just for ritual or magical purposes—a cloak, robe, belt, or dress perhaps? What if the magic wasn't reserved just for those special pieces but was something you applied to your everyday wear?

Colors, patterns, textures, and shapes can all impact how clothes look on our body—and most especially how we feel. We might feel powerful or heavy in dark colors, vulnerable or light in pastel colors, exposed or hidden by prints, luxurious or weighed down in velvet. How you feel depends so much on *you*. Consider your favorite outfits—why are they your faves? Is it the way your body looks, how comfortable the outfit feels, where you got it from, or because you love the color or the design on it? There is no wrong answer. But if you think a little more about that favorite outfit, you can start to consciously collect pieces that magically suit your needs and personality. You can create a chart of how colors, fabrics, or design elements make you feel, and start dressing inspired by that magical chart. For example, if you feel the color black makes you feel protected, then select that on days when you need a little more help. If dark blue makes you feel powerful, then it would be the ideal color to wear for your big presentation.

Clothing can be a source of stress, though, in so many ways. Maybe you've lost or gained weight so clothes aren't fitting you correctly at the moment. The budget is super tight, space is very limited, or allergies complicate what you can wear. Trying on clothes can be a nightmare that is extremely frustrating and stressful or even panic-inducing for some. Basically options can be limited and clothing-emotion associations can be complex, so you may find the suggestion above problematic—I get it.

It's times like these when I focus on something I can have with me regardless: jewelry. Be it a bracelet, ring, necklace, pendant, or pin, jewelry is one of the most adaptable and accessible things we can use for daily magic. I'm not talking fancy precious metals either—even just a braided string or ribbon can have power. Something that you can wear every day or put on before you leave the house becomes a part of you. I seriously feel out of sorts when I somehow manage to make it out the door without a certain pendant around my neck, one to two evil eye bracelets on my right wrist, and earrings. If I'm up to doing bigger things that involve dealing with a lot of people, I'll stack rings on my fingers and the necklace count goes up.

Full disclosure: as a Gemini, I once read that we are prone to "excessive adornment." In contrast to Coco Chanel's "take one thing off before you leave the house" rule, I'm more likely to put one more thing *on*. I love shiny things, and I was a professional jewelry designer for years (and still make shiny things now).

Jewelry can have a lot of magical meanings, depending on the piece and how/when we're wearing it. A ring may symbolize group membership, or you might select certain stones because you feel they help balance your mood. You may have a cherished piece given to you by a loved one that you wear every day for protection. Whether we wear jewelry to adorn, honor, remember, represent, identify, protect, inspire, or embellish, we're making it another layer of ourselves.

☉ WITCHUAL ☽
Consecration

You can bless a piece of jewelry to have a specific focus or consecrate some-thing to be worn in special circumstances. Gather the object and the elements described, perform the 3 Breaths, and create your space.

As you direct the piece of jewelry through incense or smoke or use focused breath, say the following:

> *I bless this _____ (piece of jewelry) with the power of breath of air.*

As you pass the item through or near a candle flame, say:

> *I bless this _____ (piece of jewelry) with the power of flame of fire.*

As you sprinkle water on the item, say:

> *I bless this _____ (piece of jewelry) with the power of cleansing water.*

As you sprinkle earth or salt on the item or touch it with an herb special to you, say:

> *I bless this _____ (piece of jewelry) with the power of mighty earth.*

Now hold the piece of jewelry to your heart and say:

> *With Witch's spirit, this _____ (piece of jewelry) is blessed!*

Enchanting the Tongue

What we put in our mouth feeds our temple. Food and drink not only nour-ishes our physical body but can also delight both our mind and mouth. In another sense, what comes out of our mouth can build or damage our temple (and others) depending on how we use it. We'll address each in turn.

✳ Savor Country ✳

Taste can be a very sensual experience when we take the time to pay attention. Our taste buds can detect at least five basic taste qualities: sweet, sour, salty, bitter, and umami (savory). We can also detect texture and temperature with our tongue. Scientists have proposed that our sense of taste developed as a means of survival, helping us distinguish between foods that are beneficial and those that may make us ill or worse.

Cooking is absolutely a magical process that I think is a skill everyone should learn if they're physically able. But for the following exercise, you can work with simple ingredients that might already be sitting around your kitchen.

The goal of this exercise is to sit down and savor different flavors, and chart your sensory response to them. As you taste, write down your experience with each flavor. In the future, when you're looking to create a ritual experience, you can look back and see if any of these tastes and related sensations fit your plans. Using ingredients that you've already built a relationship with not only is convenient but generally helps to provide a consistent experience and reliable results as well.

Gather: Honey, lemon, cinnamon, dark chocolate, arugula, basil, sea salt, black pepper, parmesan cheese. These I recommend trying for starters—and you need only the smallest taste to try them. If you are allergic to any, then wisely avoid those and substitute something else. Have a bottle of purified water on hand to cleanse your palate in between each tasting. Other suggestions include rosemary, lavender, cardamom, ginger, fresh mint, paprika, cumin, turmeric, and sumac. Feel free to see what else your spice cabinet or garden might yield for a taste sample.

Journal and Taste: Write down the name and origin of each ingredient. Examples: "Basil leaf: picked this morning from my window herb garden" or "Honey: Wildflower blend purchased from Blessed Bees at the 5 Points Farmers' Market, August 5, 2019." Describe what you physically see, smell, feel, and anything else you may sense *before* tasting. Give approximately thirty seconds to a minute for each taste. Take your time; this isn't an experience to rush. Consider how it feels in your mouth or the tip of your tongue. Write down what comes to mind as you taste. Your notes might include colors or images, emotions you may feel, anything it reminds you of—whatever pops into your head! Before you move on to the next item, remember to cleanse your palate.

Tongue Twisting

Now, that second part about things coming off our tongues and out of our mouths—there's some power to be explored here as well. Consider the following sayings:

> *Whatever is in the heart will come up to the tongue.* —Persian proverb
>
> *Better slip with foot than tongue.* —attributed to Benjamin Franklin
>
> *A knife wound heals, but a tongue wound festers.* —Turkish proverb

There's also the phrase "tongues will wag," which refers to gossip. From a less delicate point of view, the digestive track is one long tube that begins with our mouth and ends with our anus. It brings to mind a line from the movie *Moonstruck*, where Olympia Dukakis's character, Rose, says, "My mother has a saying: […] Don't shit where you eat." By this quirky wisdom, when we gather communally to share meals and information, we should take care not to pollute the space with words that can harm.

We're reminded of finding our voice with our Witch Lungs, and the responsibility that goes along with that power. There are definitely dangers to be considered with how and when we use our voice. Words can be damaging when we use them carelessly or especially with the intent to hurt someone. Sometimes we're angry or hurt, so we lash out without thinking. We can even direct this at ourselves, disparaging our own body and mind. Whether the words are directed externally or internally, they can do emotional and mental harm. Inversely, words can offer a world of benefits: healing, directing, guiding, opening up communication, making new friends. These kinds of words build ourselves and others up.

☉ WITCHUAL ☉
Tongue Charms

Here are two opposing charms, one to quiet the noise and another to amplify the voices that need it. These can be recited on their own or included with other kinds of spellcraft such as candles, poppet work, woven charms, or kitchen witchery.

A Charm for Quieting Tongues

Loud tongues that wag and mouths too sharp
Shall now be quiet as a carp.
Water muffled without sound
Buried deep below the ground.

A Charm for Empowering Tongues

Those whose voices have been silenced too long
I call upon spirits to make them strong.
May they be heard and their message ring true
Unblock closed ears to let their words come through.

Building the Temple Within

Think about what happens when we eat something. Typically we take a bite out of something with our teeth, and as we chew, the taste buds located all over our tongue send signals to our brain. We're aware of the size, density, and texture—getting a sense of when it's safe to swallow. After swallowing, the food travels down to our stomach, where it's broken down by the acids present, then sent through the small intestine, where the nutrients are absorbed. The waste is collected in the large intestine and then directed out the anus when our body lets us know it's time.

What we take into our bodies can nourish and sustain us, but it can also harm us if we're not careful. There's the saying "we are what we eat," which is very true down to the atomic level. Our digestive system absorbs the nutrients from what we eat and drink, using it to build and replenish cells, supporting our bodily systems. Our gut is also responsible for disposing of the leftover waste. But the process of eating isn't enough to sustain us—we must have a balanced diet to get the proper amount of nutrients. Too much of anything, even something technically healthy for us, can cause an imbalance that leads to illness. The same is true of deficiencies.

Our body often tells us what we need through cravings, once we learn to properly pay attention to it mindfully. As children we seek out sweet things to boost our energy and, left to our own devices, are likely to give ourselves a bellyache. (I once ate a whole bag of Skittles when I was about five years old, like the family-size bag. That was truly regrettable, and I couldn't even look at a Skittle for years.) As we grow older, things often become too sweet for us as our taste buds change. We surprise ourselves with the fact that we really do want to eat a salad—that spinach looks great because our body is craving iron. When I'm at an event performing, teaching, and vending, it's crucial that I get a major source of protein daily, or I'll be sure to get sick immediately after the event. When I lived in Seattle, mushrooms became a staple in our everyday diet, as they're rich in vitamin D, which is a common deficiency for people who live in areas where sunlight is limited. You might find that you're suddenly craving citrus because you're low in vitamin C. When I started eating an avocado a week, I noticed a positive change in the general health of my skin and nails. Truly, when we pay attention to our bodies, they are absolutely telling us what we need.

Eating healthy means eating what your body needs. I'm not here to prescribe to anyone what they should and should not be eating, because every *body* is different. It's a slippery slope to assign moral characteristics to someone's diet, because their bodily needs, preferences, and economic reality are their business. I know what works for me, and when it comes to Witchcraft, the authentic practice is the one that will work for you.

Ideally, what we consume will be sustainable, ethically grown, and harvested in a way that's beneficial for the land and the people raising the food and affordable for everyone involved, be it plant, animal, or mineral. Everything is interwoven—monocultures are unhealthy for the environment, regardless of what's being produced. Chemical pesticides kill beneficial insects, and if you view the world through an animistic lens, then all life is worthy of respect. The reality is we all must consume in order to live, and death is a natural part of that cycle. It comes down to what you feel is best for your beliefs, your body, and your impact on the world.

What we eat and drink can also be a metaphor for the information we take in from the world around us. From books and movies to news and conversations, we are always absorbing content in some way. They say that variety is the spice of life, so making sure we diversify our sources of information creates a more balanced approach.

What if we slowed down and considered the information we are presented with on a daily basis, as if we were eating it. Where does it come from and how did it get to us? What about it has drawn your interest, making it appealing? What size bite are you taking—too much or too little? Is it easy to bite or spoon in, or is it tough and chewy? What is the nature and mood of it? Do you need to do further research to break it down, or do you fully grasp it as is? Is the content harmful or helpful? What is worthwhile to make note of, and what do you wish to discard? Flush the shit away.

In this fast media age with a whole lot of people with a stake in the influence game, from corporations to governments, it can be far too easy to "grab and go" and end up with information that's half-baked or downright poisonous and inedible. Ask yourself, who benefits from my reaction to this material—how and why?

So whether you're consuming food or information, try to be mindful of your choices. You will feel better, both inside and out.

I Could Pee on That

I have the urge to cover something that has long had magical associations: urine. It's a natural end product of the body, and it's something humans have been paying attention to for a very long time, whether we like to think about it or not. That's mainly because the bladder is a funny thing. It is sensitive to when we are excited or fearful—which is a curious phenomenon, as generally those two extreme emotions have similar effects on the body, but how they are interpreted depends on the brain. Our bladder is less dependable at both ends of the age spectrum, as well as when we're drunk—feeding into a bunch of social complications.

Urine historically has had a lot of functional uses after it has left the body. It has been used to soften leather and makes a very effective mordant for dyeing cloth. Humans have also long used animal bladders for storage bags as well as cooking vessels. If you've ever had a pet, you're likely to know that animals—especially male mammals—use urine to mark their territory. (My friend Kace calls walking their dog "delivering the pee-mail.")

But even more fascinating is urine as a magical component. Urine has been used for cursing, protection, and counter-cursing, as well as love and fertility spells. The latter may be a surprise to you. But when you think back to marking territory with urine and the fact that pregnancy tests involve peeing on a stick, then suddenly the connection makes a lot more sense. An aggressive love spell is essentially claiming ownership over someone's heart. There are pheromones that can be present in urine that may indicate how fertile a female is.

With spells using urine for cursing or counter-cursing, we most commonly encounter the witch bottle. A witch bottle is a vessel typically made of glass or pottery and filled with urine, along with nails, pins, and other sharp objects. The lore will vary depending on the region and tradition, but the general idea is that the bottle protects a home and its residents from baneful magic, especially if it's hidden or otherwise buried on the property by the people seeking protection from spirits or from someone in a physical body trying to curse them. The urine essentially marks the territory, and the sharp objects inside the bottle fight off anyone seeking to cause harm. There are also variations where the same exact concoction is used to throw a curse at someone, so I guess it's all how you look at it. I feel this begs the question, "If I pee on this, does that mean I'm owning it or cursing it?"

There are many other spells (ancient through modern) that list urine as an ingredient, but there are also plenty of spells that don't. For sure, urine is a ready and renewable resource, but once again, keep in mind that dealing with bodily fluids is messy business (not only technically but also legally) in the sense of being a health hazard.

Magical Maintenance

You may be stressed thinking about all of the things you may need to pay attention to in order to get through life. Most of the time it's just a matter of being a little more present when going about your daily tasks. Here are some things you can do regularly with a little magical twist.

Wash Your Face with Cold Water

After I take a bath or shower, I splash cold water on my face and gently dry it before I do anything else. It can't "close the pores," as some people claim, but it does cool the surface temperature of my skin, cutting back on excess sweat and oil. It also just feels refreshing.

Magical focus: Think, "I am present in my body."

Drink When You're Thirsty

You may have heard of the "eight by eight" rule (drinking eight eight-ounce glasses of water a day), but that's another myth. The best guide is to drink when you feel thirsty. Always have fresh water on hand to drink, and opt for that instead of soda. Add lemon or lime slices if you're looking for a little more flavor.

Magical focus: Craft a sigil for your bottle of water and draw it on with an indelible marker. The sigil can be centered on hydration, or you can change it out regularly for one that represents what you need to work on. Every time you drink from the bottle, you're enhancing that connection.

Light Moisturizer and Sunscreen

I stay away from heavily scented moisturizers and those that make all sorts of claims about what they can do for your skin. Simple is better (and usually less expensive). By sunscreen, I mean using appropriate protection for your particular skin type—be that a lotion, hat, long sleeves, scarves, etc. It's worthwhile to do some research on sunblocks, because many are not environmentally friendly or effective for all skin types.

Magical focus: When applying lotion, take this time to feel your face and essentially bless yourself, saying, "May I think wisely, see purely, breathe inspiration, and speak truly."

Nail Care

Not everyone has the time, money, or desire to go to a nail salon. But everyone can benefit from a little time with an emery board and some hand cream on a regular basis. Whether you keep your nails short or long, take a moment to check in with them at least once a week. Make sure they're clean and free of dirt, file them gently to the desired shape or length, and massage in some cream that promotes healthy cuticles. If you work with your hands a lot, the cream can definitely help reduce hangnails and injuries.

Magical focus: Take this time to appreciate your nails and say thank you. Bring the cream down each finger to the knuckles and palm, and give yourself a little massage.

Hair and There

Even if I'm not planning on leaving the house, I still take a moment to brush my hair. It marks a transition for me mentally that I'm ready to start the day. You could argue that brushing the hair stimulates the scalp, so maybe that's part of it. I find shampooing and conditioning an invigorating experience as well, though that is something I do every few days. I take the time to smell the aroma of the product, massage my scalp, and rinse thoroughly. (I recognize that not everyone has hair they can brush or easily wash, so I invite you to find something that works for you instead.)

Magical focus: Whether performing basic care or getting ready for a big event, take a few moments to acknowledge being physically present in your skull. Let your fingers caress the length of your hair and visualize power emanating out to the ends.

Familiar Fabulosity

Now that we've had a good look around the temple and considered some basic maintenance plans, I want to introduce you to somewhat of a radical practice. It's a philosophy that I have personally been working to include more in my daily temple life. I call it "summoning the familiar fabulosity," also known as "use the pretty soaps and good china, damn it."

I have a tendency to want to hold on to nice things and "save" them. I don't quite know where that trait comes from, though I suspect it's genetic, emerging from a long line of little Jewish and Italian grandmothers who love a good wrapped fancy soap on display and still bemoan the loss of one plate of fine china that a cousin broke thirty years ago. But fancy soaps and fine china are best enjoyed when used sooner rather than later, just like life. A little bit of fabulosity inserted into daily life can bring moments of simple joy that are truly magical.

There's nothing inherently wrong with wanting to save things for special occasions. But you can sometimes get too wrapped up in preserving things for later rather than living in the now. The desire to hold on to things is a trait common to folks who have experienced poverty, stress, and other kinds of loss firsthand. You become afraid of more loss, of not having enough, of somehow losing out. So you might save everything, just in case. The nice things are kept in plastic, waiting. Truly some things are worth saving, but other things can become stale and expired if you wait too long to enjoy them.

As I grappled with the very unexpected death of an amazing and vivacious friend in late 2020, I was reminded that death can come for us at any time. The best thing you can do is live life to the fullest to the best of your ability. So get dressed up for no reason, make Tuesday a special occasion to celebrate something random, don't save that wine until it turns to vinegar, and don't make excuses for shit people/crappy relationships. Life is too fucking short for that nonsense. Love your temple by celebrating it not just on scheduled days but whenever your spirit calls for it.

Practical Love

It's easy for me to tell you to love your body, but I know that the task at hand can be quite a challenge. It takes time and work, but the weird thing is that one day you will realize you're actually doing it. Practicing small acts of kindness toward yourself (and others), doing self-care that addresses the whole of you, healing visible and invisible wounds—these are all part of the magic of the Lovers card. You are in a relationship with yourself.

You are also in a relationship with your body, your magic, the world around you, the spirits, ancestors, deities, etc. Essentially you are technically in a relationship with your practice. That may sound weird, but bear with me here. You likely think of your magical practice as something you do. But what if you stop to consider your practice as an entity unto itself—that it has a spirit or consciousness of its own, your partner in discovering the universe. Furthermore, your practice loves you. It loves the idea of you—not only you right now, but past you and future you as well. Your practice hums the song that calls to your Witch anatomy. Your practice knows you are up to the task. Sometimes it is waiting patiently and sometimes it wants you to hurry things up. Regardless, your practice revels in the experience of you. Once you start to consider your practice in this way, there is the potential for a dramatic shift that takes everything to the next level.

Being in a relationship with your practice may sound daunting and complicated, but it doesn't need to be—at all. Steer away from looking at only the big moments of high ritual to define your practice. Sabbats, fancy regalia, and wild, ecstatic rides all have their place, but they're not the whole of being a Witch. Instead, fall in love with the everyday small moments in between: the first scent of spring in the air, the sound as you strike a match to light a candle, the warmth of a soothing tea as it goes down your throat—all the little things found within the heart of a Witch's practice.

Also, let go of any preconceptions you have about love that may be limited to paper hearts, "love and light," or media-driven tropes. Love is nothing to roll your eyes at, nor is it limited to certain situations or people. Love is a force, part of magic itself—weaving the threads, driving the pattern, and holding the space between the threads. Love is a sense of wholeness without demanding perfection. When you start to see with your Witch's Heart, you open yourself to new possibilities.

You truly start to love your practice, and together you fully embody the whole of you. You feel and know that everything is interwoven. Your perceptions of and interactions with the world around you are enhanced. You know that magical practice is not separate from living, nor is it a hobby or a distraction. Love is your very breath. It flows in your blood and stirs in your belly. It is the bones that hold you up and the spirit that guides you. Let yourself love your practice, because it already loves you wholly and completely—and it always has.

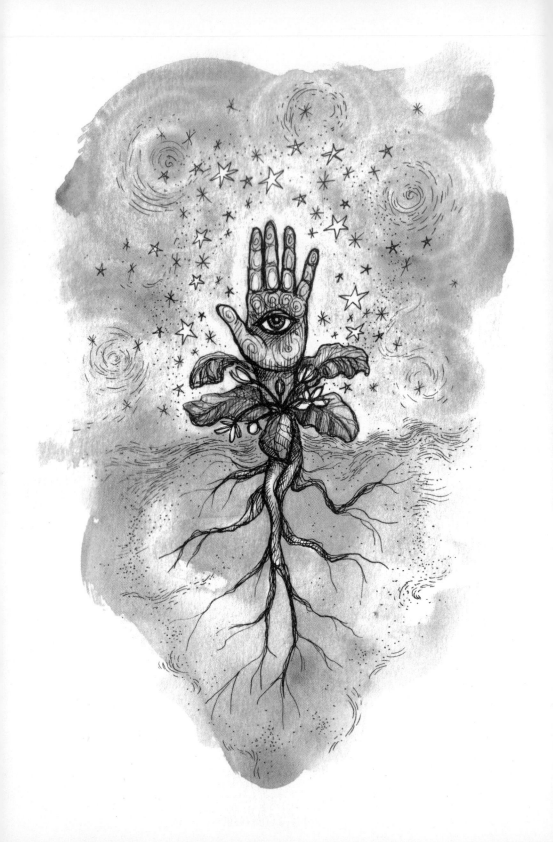

Chapter 7

Touch the Sky, Kiss the Earth

Arms and legs, hands and feet, fingers to toes,
Where my body leads is where my heart goes.
I dance the ancestors of ancient past,
A spirit vessel in the universe vast.
Ever in motion, every step a beat,
Serpents kissing where the crossroads meet.

Our hands and feet are designed to be amazing interfaces for us to experience and interact with the world. A multitude of nerve endings are present in them, constantly informing our brains about temperature, sensation, density, proximity, and so forth. With our hands we can connect and help one another, shaping the world around us. Feet help put our bodies in motion. Through them, we kiss the ground and make our way through the world. The hands and feet are critical points where the body ends and our potential to physically influence and interact with the web begins. They aid us in bringing movement and direction to the magical body.

As both an artist and a dancer, my hands and feet feel integral to my work. I have danced with headgear and costuming that significantly impacted my vision, so I had to rely on my feet to show me the way. I can't have very long nails or fancy manicures because I'm extremely tactile in my painting and sculpting practices. I need to feel my way around clay and metal, and rub my fingers to the paint and charcoal to make the marks I desire. My hands paint and craft the vision my eyes and heart wish to see in the world.

My hands and feet aren't special or more talented than anyone else's. Your hands and feet can also manifest amazing things, in your own way. This chapter will guide you in connecting more powerfully with your hands and feet—and, by association, the rest of your body as well. Getting physical (to the best of your ability) and putting your body in motion for ritual and spellcraft will yield powerful results—and you don't have to be an artist or a dancer to do it.

The Chariot
Gayly forward motion.

The Lovers have helped you to become more intimately familiar with your body—to honor your temple. You have learned about creating harmony, focusing on maintenance and preparing for movement. The Chariot asks you to get in and go, putting ideas in practice to achieve balance. For your body is not meant to be idle—it's designed for movement!

The Chariot is aligned with the number 7 and represents triumph and balance. Seven is an especially powerful number of manifestation. It may seem strange that an odd-numbered card would represent balance, but remember to "maintain balance" is not about keeping everything neat and tidy. Balance is about creating union between opposites and making unifying actions. Think about the possible combinations of earlier cards that could get us here: the Magician (1) + the Lovers (6), the Empress (3) + the Emperor (4), or the Priestess (2) + the Hierophant (5). What could each of those combinations symbolize for you at this point?

Movement can be scary—you may be afraid that you will lose control or be judged. What if you think you have two left feet or always seem to be dropping things? The Chariot reminds you that these fearful obstacles can be overcome through determination, focus, and willpower. Get in, Witch. We're going dancing!

The Ecstasy of Dance

Dance is a topic that makes a lot of people uncomfortable. Most of us danced easily as children—as well as painted, sang, and explored ourselves freely. Then we learned to feel shame, to be self-conscious of ourselves and concerned with being ridiculed because we had expressed and essentially exposed ourselves. When we let those feelings and ideas overpower us, we lose our ability to find joy and freedom in dance.

Whether we find dance acceptable or not tends to have much to do with our upbringing and larger culture. The majority of disconnection from dance likely spawned from the numerous religious sects that have considered dance sinful. All too often in these doctrines, we find the body is scorned and beaten as a means to subject people and control them. When society restricts the body, our power and spirit become limited and bound. When the body is free, the spirit is empowered and we are reminded of our connection with the world around us. Dance doesn't separate us from the divine, it connects us.

I love how Maria-Gabriele Wosien describes dance as ritual: "The dance is total surrender. In this way, the body, in the whole range of its experience, is the instrument for the transcendent power, and this power is encountered in the dance directly, instantly and without intermediaries."[20]

Even if you have trouble connecting dance to the divine, consider the basic mechanics of movement. As we age, the less we move as adults, the more difficult we find our bodies to be. There's that old adage "move it or lose it." We don't have to be doing aerobics or running a mile daily to get our bodies moving. Throughout the day you should be getting away from your desk or current position to shake things up a bit. It could be fun and refreshing to give yourself a dance break, midday or when you get home. You'll find your mood lightened and perspective shifted enough to help you focus.

---

20. Wosien, *Sacred Dance*, 9.

Touch the Sky

Think of all of the amazing things hands can do. They can grasp a tool, draw, paint, caress and soothe, pet, punch, and even speak. The hand protects, guides, instructs, stops, identifies, beckons, directs.

The power of the hand is evident through its rich use in symbolism from around the world. We have painted our hands on the walls of caves since humanity's earliest days, likely to make our presence known. Hand gestures relay messages of protection and warding through the Hand of Fatima (or hamsa), mano figa, and mano cornuta. Palm readers explore the shape and lines of our hands to peek into our destinies. The laying on of hands is believed to heal through reiki and massage. The dubious Hand of Glory is said to bring invisibility. Indian dancers use mudras to tell sacred stories.

Don't have a ritual tool handy? Your hand can be a wand to stir and direct energy, an athame to cut and signal with, a cup to hold, or a pentacle to build with or on.

When we restrict magic to just the workings of our mind, we miss out on utilizing the power our hands can harness. Our hands can manipulate and touch the invisible and unknown just as well as (if not sometimes better than) the known physical. Yet far too often we ignore or disregard them in favor of external aids.

The following exercise will help you find the power present in your hands.

✳ Reach for the Kittens: ✳ How to Activate Your Hands

You can sit or stand for this exercise, though if you are seated, it's best if you can be as upright as possible for maximum lung efficiency and effect.

Begin with the 3 Breaths exercise.

Make sure your rib cage is positioned centrally over your body (not leaning forward or back), with your shoulders relaxed and gently back, sternum lifted. It should feel a bit like your rib cage is floating and that light is emanating from your breastbone. This will mean that you are in a good posture and able to breathe as deeply as possible.

Next, lift and expand your arms out to your sides in the space roughly between your hips and shoulders. Make sure to start the movement from your armpits, radiating to upper arms, then to your elbows, wrists, palms, and fingers versus lifting your hands and letting the rest of the arm follow. This allows for movement that is actively initiated by muscle and promotes deeper body awareness. As you breathe in, raise your arms upward, and let them flow back down to your sides as you exhale.

Now I'm going to introduce you to some animal friends that are going to help you out with this exercise. First imagine that there is a stack of sleeping kittens on both sides of you (or something else you might enjoy touching). These are your Wall Kittens (see illustration). Reach out to pet the kittens softly with your fingertips. This may seem like a silly concept, but remember that imagination and play are powerful. As you reach out to engage the kittens (originating the movement from your core), you are engaging your entire arms and awakening multiple senses.

Still utilizing the same posture in your torso, initiate movement of your arms directly upward, again starting from the shoulder/armpit area. Allow your head and chin to follow upward as well. Activate your fingertips this time by picturing a giant floating bunny rabbit above you. This is the Sky Bunny. Extend your arms upward to reach for the bunny while also thinking about keeping yourself rooted (into your tailbone if you're seated, or all the way to your feet if you're standing). In this position you are connecting earth to sky and sky to earth—as above, so below. Far too often I've seen folks raise their arms limply, like they're self-conscious or just simply unaware of where their arms are. The resulting impression looks like they are being held at gunpoint, doing a crappy job of making antlers of their hands, or failing at catching a football. It doesn't complete the circuit. When you fully engage your body from head to toe, you are far more successful at conducting the energies around and through you.

Diagram of the Wall Kittens, Sky Bunny, and Floor Ferrets

Once you get what the above/below position feels like, slowly bring your arms down, petting the Wall Kittens with your fingers as they descend, palms facing down. Once your palms are about forty-five degrees from the ground, hold this position. Your overall body shape should look like an *A*. Here, your animal friends are the Floor Ferrets. Instead of reaching to pet them like you did the kittens or bunny, your job here is keep them at bay—like you're stopping them from climbing up your pants or skirt, as ferrets are wont to do. This position actually helps us work with the energy of the earth.

If you're not used to moving a lot, be sure to roll your shoulders in circles forward and back before and after this exercise. You can also shake out your arms and hands regularly as you try each position.

Lastly, connect all the positions together in a graceful cycle: kittens, bunny, ferrets and around again. Pay attention to how each position feels as you connect with it.

Gestures of the Hands

The hands can be extremely useful in channeling and directing energy. There is a reason why so many dance forms have specific hand gestures—they not only often have (or once had) symbolic meaning and add visual complexity but also direct the feeling of the dance. The language of dancing hands is a global phenomenon that is worth observing.

In classical Indian dance, there are over fifty mudras that depict aspects of the gods and other beings, helping to describe key characteristics and activities. In the guedra, a Tuareg blessing dance found primarily in Morocco, a gentle flicking of the fingers, led by the middle finger, directs energy from the dancer's heart to whatever is being blessed. In Maori dance, a closed-finger/open-palm configuration where the palms are parallel to each other (like holding a box) while the hands shake slightly in a controlled, vibrating manner is used to build up and move energy. Romani dances typically incorporate a variety of hand gestures, including cutting motions across the chest and arms, bumping various parts of the torso and hips with a fist, and wringing motions (picture wringing out a wet garment)—all accenting both the body and the music. In flamenco, there are "hand flowers" that direct the flow of movement inward or outward with a cascade of fingers and rotation of the wrist. They may sound delicate in nature, but the effect is one of strength and power.

As a geeky dancer, I have spent many hours studying as much folkloric and cultural dance as possible. Dance is an amazing gateway, as it's an opportunity to learn and share often without the barriers of language or politics. Through dance, one learns about the music, history, artistry, and spirituality of a given people or practice. There is so much nuance that can be understood through dance, and experiences can be shared and exchanged. When I'm teaching dance, one of my favorite things is that others often love to share their own experiences from their backgrounds. We can compare, contrast, and exchange concepts to explore for our personal practice. That's not to say anyone becomes an expert on someone else's movements through a short demonstration, but it does help us explore what's possible for ourselves and consider how or why something works. It's especially fascinating not just to see the differences between dance movements but also to discover the larger number of commonalities that have developed often independently around the world.

Common Hand Positions[21]

- *Fist:* Closes/contains energy within the body
- *Open hand, spread fingers:* Welcoming, extends outward, receiving
- *Open palm, fingers closed:* Also receiving or offering, but directs energy more specifically
- *Hands coming from the head:* Directing spiritual energy from the mind
- *Hands coming from the chest:* Directing emotional and connective energy
- *Hands coming from the belly:* Directing physical healing, fertility, and well-being
- *Palms out:* Offering or sending energy outward
- *Palms in:* Directing or sending energy inward

---

21. These hand positions are not exactly universal—there are cultural nuances to take into consideration. For example, showing an open palm might be seen as a gesture of welcome in many places, but in some cultures that same hand gesture might be considered offensive or taboo.

- *Arms and palms up:* Connecting with the sky, invoking or drawing in
- *Arms and palms down:* Connecting with the earth, releasing or resting

Kissing the Earth

When you move with both confidence about yourself and compassion for the impact your body makes, I call this "kissing the earth with your feet." A powerful person does not have to pound the ground with every step. When you think about it, stomping can be disrespectful to the earth as well as harmful to your body (for every action there's a reaction).[22] Whether I'm teaching dance or basic ritual movement technique, I always start with the feet.

Your feet are your connection to the ground and the receivers of the effects of gravity on your body. The three primary parts of your feet that are directly involved in the process are your toes, balls, and heels. Most people tend to walk with the heel making first contact with the ground, followed by the ball and toes. I instruct my students to reverse the order, which is better for your body by lessening the impact. If you often deal with knee, hip, and back pain, changing how you walk can reduce those pains greatly as well as improve your balance and general mobility. When you walk from heel to toe, you are putting the full force of your weight onto your heel. The heel really doesn't have a lot of cushion to it, so the impact with the ground reverberates up your body with every step while also taking away the stabilizing benefits of your toes. This way of walking also means there's no room for correction if you misstep, and your ability to rebalance yourself is greatly reduced. However, when you walk toe-ball-heel, you can ease your weight onto each foot more effectively, cushioning each step. It's also easy to course-correct because you haven't committed your entire weight to your foot until the heel hits the ground.

Most of the time when I perform dance, I am barefoot (if allowed and the surface is safe). I choose to do this because the exposure essentially gives me "eyes" on my feet, because I can't be looking at the floor when I've got an audience

---

22. There are forms of dance and music where stomping is involved. They generally involve proper footwear, body training, and/or staging to avoid damaging the body.

to engage with. I'm using those nerve receptors on my feet to sense if there's anything out of the ordinary, such as unexpected wetness, an instrument cable, something sharp, uneven floorboards, pasta, etc. When I sense a potential threat, all I have to do is move my foot somewhere else, because I haven't fully stepped yet. Shoes, on the other hand, may not alert me like my bare toes can to cables that are about to trip me or uneven footing. However, if I know the stage or area is going to be especially hazardous, dirty, etc., I'll take the risk and wear shoes.

✳ Hello, Feet! ✳

Note: This exercise is most effective when done from a standing position, but if you have balance or mobility issues, you can certainly perform it from a seated position.

Start with saying hello to your feet. (Really, when was the last time you acknowledged your feet and all the work they do?)

Take a moment to consider what the ground feels like through your feet. Even if you're wearing shoes or socks right now, you should have a sense of what the floor feels like. Is there a squish of carpet, the soft bounce of wood, or the cool density of stone or concrete? Can you sense what temperature it is?

Next gently rock your body from side to side, allowing the weight to shift from one foot to the other. You can lift your foot up if that helps as the weight comes off it and onto the other foot.

Now rock your body forward and back, feeling the weight move from your toes and balls to your heels. Think about how your body feels on top of your feet and how the earth feels below them.

Once you've got that sorted out, it's time to walk. Just like how I instructed you earlier in this chapter when you learned to activate your hands, with the movements of the arms and hands being initiated from the shoulders / armpit region, intentional movement of the feet starts up where the leg meets the hip. Feel the top of your thigh—the muscles most responsible for movement are your quadriceps, which are situated on the top and side of each leg. Balancing these out on the back sides of your legs and up into your buttocks are the glutes (you can feel your butt up here if you'd like).

Begin by standing with your feet approximately shoulder-width apart, weight evenly distributed. Now shift your weight over to your left side so that your right leg is free to move. Starting from the right hip, pick up your right leg and move it slightly forward (basically not a huge step, but a comfortable small step), and focus on letting your toes make contact with the ground first, followed by the ball and lastly the heel. As the heel makes contact with the ground, you should be shifting your weight completely to the right side, freeing up your left leg to now move forward. Touch with the left toe, ball, and heel.

Now the next thing you need to do is look forward instead of at your feet. (How did I know you were looking at your feet??)

Proceed in a small circle, taking your time with small, easy steps—keeping your head and torso centered as you move forward.

Whether you're moving around your home, taking the dog for a walk, or running errands, take a moment to think about how you're moving. Put in the effort to think about kissing the earth. I guarantee you will find it easier to move over time and will likely even feel fewer aches and pains.

✶ Altaring the Body: ✶ Circle-Casting with Movement

In the Witch Lungs chapter, you learned how to create magical space within your body. Now that you have learned to engage your hands and feet, you are ready to learn about using your body to cast a circle. From invoking the elements to welcoming in deity/spirits/ancestors, your body will lead the way. While many people recite words and use specific ceremonial gestures and tools when casting a magic circle, you can do this method without saying a single word (if you'd like) with just your body. You can also use this approach to make your casting as simple and quick—or as long and theatrical—as you'd like.

Note: Depending on your mobility, the availability of accessible room for movement, and of course your ritual needs, you can do this exercise from a seated position or take up a whole space with walking/dancing.

With this method, you do not need to set up a physical altar or raise a stang (though you can if you want to, of course). Instead of the stang/altar taking up the center or a side, your body becomes the place of action and connectivity. You are the altar, the place of action, the conduit. You are present at the crossroads while also being the exact place where all of these roads meet.

If I am going to create formal ritual space outside of my body, this is how I do it.

1. I begin by taking a deep breath to pull air into my lungs while at the same time mentally focusing on the qualities of Air.[23] I may think of a gentle breeze or a cleansing wind. Besides taking a breath, I consciously raise my chest and open my arms up and outward, spreading my fingers. The visual effect is something like a tree gently swaying with the wind.

2. Next I think about Fire. I tend to localize this to my chest and hips. I visualize a candle or bonfire while my shoulders and/or hips may softly shimmy like a flame, my arms framing my body, fingers flickering.

3. I follow Fire with Water. Here I think about the ocean or a spring shower while the movement becomes more localized to my core. My arms become more fluid and horizontal in their movements while my hips softly undulate. My pelvis may move in circles or figure eights or sway from side to side—like the motion of the ocean.

4. Earth comes next. I picture forests, mountains, creatures of the land. My arms and hands focus downward as my feet kiss the earth gently. Depending on the purpose of the ritual, I may also drop my shoulders or push my hips from side to side to create a feeling of percussion.

5. Once I have acknowledged the elements, I connect to above/below as well as within/without. Building on the common metaphysical saying "As above, so below," I acknowledge all of the realms, gesturing with my arms symbolically up to the sky and heavens as well as down to the earth and underworlds. These connective movements create a central axis in the space, connecting all directions like a compass rose. To further emphasize my personal interconnection with the universe, I bring both of my hands in toward my heart while tak-

---

23. After connecting to Air, you can align the breath with each element, associate it with a color, or just not focus on it as much. Just don't forget to breathe.

ing a breath in. I then extend my arms out to embrace the world at the same level as my heart, exhaling as I reach out.

6. Lastly, if the working requires it, I connect with Spirit. This can be done by turning in a small spiral in whichever direction seems appropriate. If I am working with a specific deity, I will do movements that I feel are specific and connected to that deity. These are often inspired by the art that has been made to honor these beings over centuries. For example, the posture for Hekate is tall and strong, arms raised as if they are holding torches, crossing in the center as they move up. If I'm calling in Pan, I may jump around like a goat. That might sound silly, but it will certainly get the horned one in your space quicker than two shakes of a goat's tail.

The order in which you connect to the elements is up to you, as well as whether you'd like to connect them with certain directions. With these factors, it's important to remember two things. First, the elements surround you— you may assign them directions ceremonially, but if you go far enough into the east, you will end up in the west, and if you wander too far north you will eventually end up in the south. (Thanks, round planet!) Second, present within your body are all of the elements: air as breath, blood as water, fire in the electrical pulses of your nerves, and your flesh and bone as earth. So it's very easy for your body to address those elements within and externally—just by using movement that is intuitive for you. If what I describe doesn't feel quite right for you, do what feels good and appropriate for you.

If I am going to mark out a space bigger than my body, I will trace its circumference with my body. I might move through the space at least three times, each rotation holding symbolic meaning for me. In the first pass, I mark the circle on the physical plane with my feet. In the second pass, I mark the circle visually with my mind. I bring the circle into spiritual space in the third pass. I am also linking past (first pass), present (second pass), and future (third pass) while I align the body, the mind, and the spirit. Then, from the center, I begin working with the elements and spirits, turning in place as I address each.

You can do this all in silence, or you can have music to accompany you. I have a selection of pieces of mostly instrumental music that vary in length from one minute to ten minutes, depending on what I need.[24] I also work with live musicians on occasion.[25]

When I'm done with my work, I don't have to retrace my steps or go through the elements and spirits all over again. Instead, I stand in the middle of my space and do a gesture of appreciation or acknowledgment that signals the end of the working. It is done.

☾ WITCHUAL ☾
Witch Direction

Clockwise (deosil) or counterclockwise (widdershins)? There is a lot of lore about which way you should move through a circle, depending on the practice and tradition. Typically I move both ways through a space, depending on what I'm doing. I see moving counterclockwise as a departure from the normal, while clockwise engages with the seasonal tides. Widdershins works well with banishing and cleansing, while healing and building energy are associated with deosil movement. The best way to find out what works for you is to move both ways and experience what they feel like.

How you move through your magical space isn't limited to circular motion either. You can move through your space like you're navigating a compass rose. For example, you could be working north-south and east-west, returning to the center or another location of significance as you go. You might acknowledge the diagonal spaces in between the cardinal directions, creating an *X* with your movements. Perhaps a working associated with the numen of a place requires you to zero in on one specific direction, so that's where you'll direct

---

24. When using recorded music, set up your ritual music on one dedicated set list, and make sure it's not on shuffle.

25. Please note that "person with a drum" does not necessarily equal "musician." Far too many people get absorbed in beating an instrument and stop paying attention to what's happening in the space or listening to musicians who may be present. When you are creating space, you want someone who is reliable, consistent, and engaged.

your attention. Maybe you're working with Underworld symbolism, so you might focus on the floor—or face upward for a higher realm.

Unsure which direction to go in? Consider the reason for your ritual, the lunar and/or solar timing, and what your intuition tells you. Folklore, mythology, and tradition can help guide you to consider which direction is best. Allow room for experimentation and don't be surprised if you accidentally move in a way you weren't planning on. Perhaps it was the right way all along.

Rose Compass

Chapter 8
Tending the Cauldrons

One cauldron in the belly below,
Warming the body so life can flow.
One cauldron in the chest tends the flame,
Sets heart in motion, eyes on the game.
One cauldron a crown over the head,
Guiding god-spirit holding the thread.

The medieval Irish bardic poem "The Cauldron of Poesy" describes three spiritual cauldrons found within the human body. The Cauldron of Warming is situated just below the navel, nestled in the pelvis where both our digestive and reproductive systems can be found. This cauldron is connected to the most primal, instinctual, animal part of ourselves—and our basic health and physical well-being. We know from the Witch Heart that the Cauldron of Motion sits in our chest near our lungs and heart. The Cauldron of Motion is named as such because the things that literally get us moving are its domain. This passionate cauldron is fueled by inspiration and is most greatly influenced by art, poetry, music, academic exploration, and emotional openness. The third cauldron is the Cauldron of Wisdom, which is found within or above the head. This cauldron is related to our spiritual development, interconnectivity, and greater wisdom.

While these cauldrons don't exist physically, working with them can have very real and powerful effects on our bodies. They help us engage with aspects of ourselves that we tend to overlook or ignore. It can be easy to address things we can readily see on the outside, but things on the inside can be much more difficult to tackle. In some ways, doing that surface work is like a car wash: it's a physical process that results in making you feel like things are back in order, and it's accessible. But working on the engine seems a bit more daunting, doesn't it? Luckily you don't need to know how to change a timing belt or catalytic converter in order to help your car's engine run better on a regular basis, though taking it in for an oil change for scheduled maintenance can definitely help. But even this simple task is something that can be ignored or put off as not as important—until something goes wrong, often causing a cascade of problems. Just like with cars, regular maintenance of the magical body can help keep you in tune and improve your body's performance.

The simplicity of the cauldrons—there being only three of them situated in places you can physically access with just a touch—makes them accessible and easier to work with than more complicated systems and models. The following exercises are designed to help you engage with each one on an individual basis. Once you become familiar with each cauldron, you can work with them collectively. All together, they help unify the body, mind, and spirit, which in turn enhances the magical body.

Strength
The body united.

The motion of the Chariot has taught you about balance and brought you vitality. As you encounter the eighth card of the major arcana, you will find out about a different kind of balance. Strength signifies being able to release your fears so that you can unite your mind, body, and soul. It speaks of physical strength combining with emotional and mental strength. Strength embodies the triumph of love over hate. The number 8, with its relation to the ever-looping infinity symbol, brings us mastery and serenity. As you learn to tend to your cauldrons, you bring strength to yourself physically and spiritually.

✳ A Ritual to Tend to Your ✳ Cauldron of Warming

Are you ready to clean the invisible cauldron that will help improve the overall health of your body? While it's not meant to be a replacement for proper food and exercise, this exercise can help remove blockages that may be damaging your health and create a deeper sense of bodily harmony.

According to the lore of "The Cauldron of Poesy," we are born with the Cauldron of Warming situated upright to help us perform basic life functions. Alas, this is the first cauldron we tend to neglect as we get older, taking it for granted. As we overload ourselves mentally, emotionally, or spiritually, we can upset this crucial cauldron, setting off a cascade of physical problems. It's amazing how much better we can feel by giving the Cauldron of Warming a little proper attention.

Start by centering yourself with the 3 Breaths exercise.

Close your eyes and place one or both hands over your abdomen (whatever feels most comfortable to you). Do a focused breath where you breathe deep into your belly.

In your mind's eye, visualize a small cauldron sitting there, just below your navel. Evaluate the state of the cauldron: What position is it in—upright, tilted on its side, or upside down? What does it look like? Is it clean and shiny, or does it feel like it could use a solid washing? Is there anything in the cauldron?

If the cauldron appears to you that it needs some TLC, take another focused breath. Then visualize adjusting, emptying, cleaning, or polishing the cauldron—whatever you think it needs—in order for it look the way you want it to. This area also responds very well not only to movement with your hands but also moving your belly and hips. Simple, easy movements could include twisting your hips back and forth (like an old upright washing machine), moving your pelvis in circles or figure eights, or gentle shimmies. Do what feels comfortable and effective for you until you are satisfied.

Lastly, place your hand(s) back over your belly (if you moved them in the previous step) and take one more focused breath. As you exhale, see the cauldron as you wish it to be: upright, clean, and full of what's important to you. When you're ready, open your eyes. The ritual is complete.

Another layer that you can add to this ritual (which can be especially helpful for folks who have trouble visualizing) is to do this with a physical cauldron. First wash and dry your vessel as befitting its material. Next, bless the cauldron. Here a suggestion for a full consecration using all of the elements: First waft the incense smoke around the cauldron, then quickly pass it through a candle flame. Next sprinkle well (or other blessed) water on and in it, followed by a light touch of some earth or salt. Dry the cauldron off and wrap it up with an altar cloth remnant or a piece of fabric that is special to you. Let it rest for three days, then place the newly blessed cauldron on your altar to use. Tend to your cauldron regularly and fill it with things that can help keep it healthy, such as stones and crystals, herbs, intentions written on scrolls, etc.

It doesn't have to be an actual cauldron either—it can be a small bowl or pot. I am especially fond of the small Japanese ceramic bowls that are often used for rice, soup, or tea, as they fit nicely in my hands, are well made, are aesthetically pleasing, and typically cost only five to ten dollars. Ceramic artists who exhibit at festivals tend to make mini-pots and bowls that are very inexpensive and unique.

Performing this ritual on a regular basis can help keep you in tune with the physical state of your body. People dealing with a lot of physical issues may want to do this exercise on a weekly or monthly basis. If you wish to help set new healthy habits, I'd recommend doing this ritual during the period from the new moon to the early crescent. If you're looking to banish some bad habits, consider performing it during the last part of the waning moon.

✳ A Ritual to Cleanse ✳ Your Cauldron of Motion

The Cauldron of Motion is essentially our engine—it contains what moves us, lighting our inner fire and fueling our passion for life. But gunk can build up in this cauldron, slowing down our momentum and drowning our enthusiasm. Often we don't even realize we're building up sludge in this vital engine, so it's essential to tend to the Cauldron of Motion on a regular basis.

Do you have a tendency to put others' needs and desires constantly in front of your own? Are you making sacrifices for others who don't value your effort or work? While it is truly a good thing to take care of other people, we have to be careful not to let other people's expectations of us override what we need for ourselves. Sometimes we replace what we need to keep us moving with the wants and needs of other people. This mode is not sustainable. In order for you to be there to help others, you need to be able to place value on your own needs and goals. Otherwise you run the risk of getting mired down, depressed, and worn out. Consider: Are you stuffing your cauldron full of other people's ideas and demands on you? Are you leaving enough room for you?

Start by centering yourself with the 3 Breaths exercise.

Close your eyes and place one or both hands over your heart (whatever feels most comfortable to you). Do a focused breath where you breathe into your sternum area.

In your mind's eye, visualize there being a small cauldron within your chest, just behind your sternum. Evaluate the state of the cauldron: What position is it in—upright, tilted on its side, or upside down? What does it look like? Is it clean and shiny, or does it feel like it could use a solid washing? Is there anything in the cauldron?

If the cauldron appears to you that it needs some TLC, take another focused breath. Then visualize adjusting, emptying, cleaning, or polishing the cauldron— whatever you think it needs—in order for it look the way you want it to. In addition to picturing your actions, you can also move your hands (and the rest of your body too if you wish) to help with the process, until you are satisfied.

Lastly, place your hand(s) back over your heart (if you moved them in the previous step) and take one more focused breath. As you exhale, see the cauldron as you wish it to be: upright, clean, and full of what's important to you. When you're ready, open your eyes. The ritual is complete.

If you have a hard time doing the visualization, this ritual can be done as a physical exploration by way of sympathetic magick. Follow the instructions from the previous ritual to bless and use a physical cauldron. You can fill your cauldron with symbols and items that you feel help generate emotional well-being.

Performing this ritual on a regular basis can help keep you balanced and focused. Consider doing it on the equinoxes and possibly the solstices as well, if you'd like to do a quarterly check-in.

✳ A Ritual to Connect with ✳ Your Cauldron of Wisdom

If we have a hard time connecting with our own sense of self, it can be even more difficult to engage with others. We may be confused about what our purpose is or if we're really making the right decisions. This ritual will help you gain clarity and connection.

Our last cauldron to engage with is the Cauldron of Wisdom, situated within the head or just above it. According to lore, we are born with this cauldron upside down—it's our challenge to right it as we grow and find our way in the world. The Cauldron of Wisdom guides our spiritual development, becoming a fountainhead that connects us to the flow of the world.

Start by centering yourself with the 3 Breaths exercise.

Close your eyes and place your hands either on the crown, the cap, or the base of your skull. Do a focused breath, inhaling up into your head.

In your mind's eye, visualize a small cauldron sitting there behind your eyes and between your ears or on top of your head. Evaluate the state of the cauldron: What position is it in—upright, tilted on its side, or upside down? What does it look like? Is it clean and shiny, or does it feel like it could use a solid washing? Is there anything in the cauldron?

If the cauldron appears to you that it needs some TLC, take another focused breath. Then visualize adjusting, emptying, cleaning, or polishing the cauldron—whatever you think it needs—in order for it look the way you want it to. You can massage your skull, gently roll your head around with your neck, or softly tilt or shake your head to stir things up.

Lastly, place your hand(s) back over your head (if you moved them in the previous step) and take one more focused breath. As you exhale, see the cauldron as you wish it to be: upright, clean, and full of what's important to you. When you're ready, open your eyes. The ritual is complete.

Remember, if you have a hard time doing the visualization, you can also follow this up by working with a real cauldron (or perhaps a skull-shaped vessel, if you find that appealing). Follow the instructions from the first ritual in this chapter (for the Cauldron of Warming) to bless and use a physical cauldron. You can fill your cauldron with symbols and items that foster connectivity, clear thinking, and positivity.

The full moon is an excellent time to perform this ritual. You can also use this ritual to help you connect more deeply with ancestors and other spirits, so Samhain is another good time for it.

✳ The Cauldron Fountain Ritual ✳

Once you have familiarized yourself with each of the three cauldrons separately, it's time to combine them and address all three cauldrons within a single ritual. Start with the Cauldron of Warming, followed by the Cauldron of Motion, and lastly the Cauldron of Wisdom. Focus on one at time, just like you did previously, but once you finish with one, move up the line to the next one. Once you have taken care of each cauldron in turn, it's time to allow them to flow into each other, like a beautiful fountain.

Let your arms rest at your sides, palms open and up, forming the base of a triangle with your head.

Take a breath into your head, visualizing the Cauldron of Wisdom bubbling up and overflowing.

Next take a breath into your chest, seeing the waters flow from above down into the Cauldron of Motion. It too in turn bubbles up and overflows.

Lastly, breathe into your belly, the stream from the upper cauldrons flowing down into the Cauldron of Warming. It receives those waters and sends blue light out to all of the edges of your body, including your hands.

Raise your arms up over your head, channeling that energy to flow up and over like a pump returning water to the top of a fountain.

Let your arms come down through the center of your body, palms facing toward you, hands spaced equally about the distance from ear to ear.

Touch each cauldron as you meet it, and repeat this motion two more times, flowing up, over, and down.

Lastly, take one more breath that draws through all three zones, and exhale slowly.

You can do this exercise whenever you feel like parts of yourself have gone astray or are discombobulated. It can be especially fun and relaxing to do this in the shower or while swimming in the ocean.

Chapter 9
Home within the Temple

Upon my brow rests a brilliant star,
A guiding light beacons from afar.
Come inside, rest your body and mind,
For within the darkness you will find
Fellow kindred and spirits of place.
Witch-woven, yours is a welcomed face.

As we wrap up our journey together, I want to send you with a few more things to adorn the inner walls of your temple—some words and some rites to help adorn the temple within. And while the number 9 does represent the Hermit, I want you to know that you are not alone. You're not the only one figuring this out, or who is into these weird things. There are many wonderful Witches out there in the world.

And in another sense, you are surrounded by spirits. Not just those encased in other human bodies, but also the spirits of place, plants, animals—as well as deities, ancestors, and other beings. That's not to say they're watching you while you're sleeping or having sex (that's what cats are awkwardly for), but you're not alone in this tapestry.

Not that you need anyone else. You are whole on your own. But it's good to know you have backup if you need it. There are kindred spirits out there in all forms, if we open ourselves to connecting with them.

So when you do feel alone or lonely, reflect upon your Witch anatomy. The universe breathes you just as much as you breathe it. You have a place and a pulse in the pattern of life. You are enchantment embodied, capable of transformation. You are the song your ancestors dreamed of. You are the Weaver, a living mystery.

The Hermit

By the powers of 3 combined.

We began our journey together with the Fool and we shall end it with the Hermit. We started at 0 and find ourselves at 9, which technically means the Hermit is the tenth card in the major arcana. Nines signal that one leg of your journey is coming to a close, so it's time to start reflecting on where you have been before you decide where to go next. If 3 represents the choices you can make, then arriving at 9 means you are looking at the results of those choices amplified. So rest for a moment and listen to the wisdom offered by the Hermit. Consider, contemplate, take stock, and examine the maps before you in the light that the Hermit offers. Then you will truly be ready to begin a new cycle.

In the cave of the Hermit you will find that body, mind, and spirit have been balanced within and without. The Hermit never retreats into their cave unprepared—they take exactly what they need with them to sustain them and to prepare them for future mysteries. The lantern the Hermit holds for you is actually the Star that lights your path to come. The light of others will also help guide your way. Accepting assistance when it is needed is never weakness, but rather being open to help speaks of courage, maturity, and strength of character. It means you will never truly lose your way because you won't fear looking bad by asking for directions. You will know that mistakes made along the way are simply guideposts that steer you toward the future. Adventure and wisdom are calling your name because you are ready and prepared.

Come into the Dark

The Hermit is beckoning you into the cave. What does it mean to accept this invitation? What are you willing to learn? What will you let go of? Are you ready to descend into the Underworld?

Caves can be scary places. When it's dark and you can't see where you're going, it's easy to become afraid. You don't know what lurks in the shadows, but your imagination might have a pretty good idea. You can't get comfortable when there's dampness and every place feels cold and hard. What if you get stuck in a tight spot? Fear, panic, and anxiety can become quite powerful in the darkness of the cave.

But caves can also be places of comfort. There are times when you need to retreat from the world, to hole up somewhere safe and hidden. If you know how to light a fire and make yourself at home, a dark and scary place can be transformed into a haven. The cave becomes a familiar place that helps you rather than vexes you. Sometimes all you want and need is to be able to turn off all of the lights and outside noises so you can look deeper within, without distraction. Nestle into the darkness and listen to the breathing of the Underworld.

Working with the Witch anatomy can be both kinds of cave experiences. Let's see what could be waiting for you in the dark. For there are healthy fears for you to have and there are parts of yourself that can act like your own worst enemy. The trick is learning the difference.

Speaking to Shadows

In recent years, I have heard so much talk of shadows and shadow selves, spreading from one corner of the internet to another, like a cloud of octopus ink in a ten-gallon aquarium. While it is fascinating to see Jungian concepts applied to Witchcraft practice,[26] there are a lot of people tripping themselves (and others) up in the process of interpretation and subsequent application. Shadow sounds spooky and the dark can definitely be scary, so it's not surprising that many people talk about the shadow self as being the so-called bad, negative, or harmful parts of themselves. But that's not really what the shadow self is.

---

26. Psychology is one way of creating and applying theory to explain life experiences. I believe that if a model or approach helps to unlock something for you, that's great. But be careful trying to use it as a skeleton key to open all of the doors to perception. One size does not fit all when it comes to human experience.

In Jungian psychology, the *shadow* is believed to be an unconscious aspect of the personality that the conscious self does not identify with or is not openly aware of. It could be the whole of our unconscious being as well—the primal, animalistic side of ourselves. Essentially, the shadow is akin to the Serpent in many ways. We know the Serpent means well, but it can be hard for us to interpret, causing frustration. Its urges and signals may make us feel uncomfortable, but that doesn't mean that discomfort is unwarranted or bad. We must work with the Weaver to interpret those signs and make the right choices for ourselves.

The unknown depths of the psyche are not automatically bad, evil, or imperfect. These deeper parts of ourselves are simply harder for us to immediately understand, as they communicate differently. That is why we need to give ourselves some grace and build a relationship with the Serpent, versus demonizing it when we make a poor choice. Nor should we paralyze ourselves with the fear of doing something wrong, or believe we must reach some perfect state before being able to do anything. Rather, the realization of those patterns is something for us to consider moving forward. Remember, know thyself—the good parts and the not-so-great ones.

It is good and difficult work to address the problematic parts of ourselves and our society. But there are two things to keep in mind:

1. Witches do magical work both because of and in spite of those parts of ourselves. As human beings, it is your job to experience, to learn, to grow, and to change. You aren't meant to be perfect and no amount of waiting will get you there. Just like with dance, you can't wait until you feel you "look good" in order to start learning how to do it. You have to move now in this moment, as the next big cue to move on is Death. Life, or a Witch's practice, is not a piece of choreography learned by watching or dictation. You have to get up and suck at it before you get to be anywhere near good. You have to figure out how it feels for yourself, without becoming paralyzed by fear of inner or outer critiques. And no matter how well you learn it, this magical dance of life is improvised, constantly changing with the music.

2. Not everything difficult is hiding in the shadows. So much of it is propped up under glaring lights, like stolen treasure displayed in a museum that so many walk right on by. Be mindful not to blame the dark, the hidden, the taboo, and the mysterious for your discomfort, whether it comes from you or others. Some of the most intense healing happens in caves of shadows, and some of the greatest damage is caused by bleaching light. One is not inherently bad while the other is solely good. Blame, shame, and their associated baggage can blind you from seeing clearly, causing wounds to fester that cloud the heart and mind.

I hope by now you understand that following the Serpentine Path is understanding that you're not striving for perfection. Perfection is like a butterfly pinned down under glass. Nobody's able to fly under those circumstances, let alone live. Instead, seek room for growth, change, and movement. Recognize the power of the things you do choose to have in your life, as well as explore the benefits of moving along things that no longer suit you.

We turn to Witchcraft to invoke change in our lives, our selves, and the world around us. Like the Serpent, we wind ourselves through and around the world, going underground and rising up again, striking and recoiling, honing our skills, shedding our skins as we grow. If we don't move, if we don't change, if we don't shed those older versions of ourselves, we stagnate and become blind to the world. Only then do we truly fail to speak to our shadow and deny the power of our Serpent.

Be Vulnerable, but Wear Protection

As a Witch you have walked a winding path to get here and likely survived many wounds along the way—big ones, small ones, bruises that you're not even sure how you got in the first place. Witchcraft is not a matter of comparing wounds, competing for who walked the hardest path, but instead of recognizing common threads, even if we're not all at the same place on our journeys. The Witch is not a victim. The power is not in the wounds, but in your ability to change in spite of them, and to keep moving forward on the path, rooted in your strength to trust yourself. You are not always going to be successful in every change you seek to make, but if you infuse your practice with compassion and vulnerability, you will definitely become more in tune with your path.

Vulnerability is another one of those scary things,[27] largely because people can be scary, even dangerous. Over the years, I have learned to become more open, communicative, compassionate, and vulnerable, both of and to myself as well as others. Vulnerability should not be confused with weakness, but rather is a willingness to explore, to change, and to be changed. To progress past those places of pain, to heal those old wounds, while remembering to be wise whenever possible. Back in my youth, I used to worry about what people thought of me. It's where I looked to for definition because I couldn't see myself in all of the mess. But then I cleared away the debris and found how to trust myself. Now I'd say my biggest fear is inadvertently hurting the people I care about. I recognize I can't control others, but I can try to be mindful of myself. It's a work in progress, as we all are.

My philosophy for people is this: Trust that humans are going to be human. We all make mistakes and we can never truly know what's going on in someone else's head. I try to keep that in mind before jumping to conclusions about what someone said or did. Folks have a tendency to throw around the phrase "perfect love and perfect trust" in Witchcraft, either with a sense of perceived pureness or while being snide about it. Neither option begins to grasp what that phrase means. Perfect trust is more about saying, "I recognize who you are and who I am, exactly in this moment." Perfect love means to recognize the good and the bad, the subjective and the objective, and the nuance in between—and the flux of change. To understand and accept responsibility for your own expectations and efforts right here, right now.

---

27. I highly recommend checking out Brené Brown's work on vulnerability. She has several great podcasts and TED talks that are free and easy to listen to, and your local library likely has at least a few of her books. Check out www.brenebrown.com.

If you are able to recognize this in yourself and others, then you are open to possibilities. You're not so open that you're unprotected or naive. The past becomes a guide, not a tether to hold you back. You can take precautions, both metaphysically and physically, to protect yourself and be prepared. How? Because your Witch Lungs have taught you both connection and sovereignty of self. Your Witch Heart has given you both vision and the ability to perceive patterns. The Serpent is prepared to act, the Bones are supporting your practice, and the Weaver is in control. You are the Witch.

Illuminate the Path

The best way to navigate your way through the darkness of the cave is by letting your vision adjust to your environment. Once the glare of the outside light has diminished and the quietude of the cave has calmed your nerves, you start to see more clearly than ever. You notice there is light in this cave, and it's not just coming from the Hermit's lantern. It comes from within you. Remember, you are a stellar body, taking your place among the stars and illuminating the world around you.

As you prepare to leave the cave to start your next journey, take with you these words from the Hermit:

> *Be vigilant and strong, but also be fluid and kind.*

> *Speak the truth, supported by compassion and wisdom.*

> *What moves within you also moves without and beyond.*

> *Be guided not only by your eyes and ears, but also by your heart, hands, and feet.*

> *May change be a blessing and an opportunity for balance on your path.*

And last but not least:

> *May your spirit always be inspired.*

Be the Witch (I Know You Are)

Be the Witch (I know you are),
Treading upon the earth.
Each step a testament to grace,
Resounding with reverence,
Fortified by presence of mind.

Be the Witch (I know you are),
Every word spoken carefully chosen,
Selected for its deeper meaning,
Intoned with your essence and
Sanctified by sound.

Be the Witch (I know you are),
Listening to the hum of the world,
Like a spider and her web:
Feeling, sensing, seeing
Every vibration of the thread.

Be the Witch (I know you are),
Knowing fingers that work worn edges,
Turning over leaf and stone,
Assembling the mysteries
That have been known.

Be the Witch (I know you are),
Touching symbols and tools
To divine future paths,
Turning over card and rune,
A gaze from the past.

Be the Witch (I know you are),
Dancing on liminal hedges,
Navigating between the worlds,
Wrapped in cloak of darkness
Yet crowned by light.

Be the Witch (I know you are),
A luminous numen of
God and animal,
Embodied vessel of flesh and spirit
And sibling of stars.

Be the Witch (I know you are),
Weaving together blood and lore.
A vision of confidence and creature,
Moss-made, antler-adorned,
Myth and magick made alive.

Be the Witch (I know you are),
Keeper of wisdom
Beautifully bound by secrets,
Revealing the truth of the world
With every kiss of earth.

Be the Witch (I know you are),
Confident, watching, knowing,
Residing in roots and flowers,
Flying with the moon and tides.
As above and so below.

✳ A Witch's Ritual of Dedication ✳

There is a sense of validation that comes with having the title of "Witch" bestowed upon you through formal training and being recognized as such by other practitioners. But as we have learned throughout this book, the only person who can truly make you a Witch is *you*.

Sometimes having a little ritual to declare that self-recognition comes in handy. A rite of dedication can help to instill a sense of formality. The word *dedicate* comes from Latin *dedicat*, meaning "devoted, consecrated."[28] So you

---

28. Lexico.com, a collaboration between Dictionary.com and Oxford University Press, s.v. "dedicate," https://www.lexico.com/definition/dedicate.

can look at this ritual as marking your devotion to following this path. A rite of dedication is an oath that you make to yourself. You can choose to do a dedication ritual on a semi-regular basis as well, such as once a year or every five years. This repetition can help you evaluate your path and refocus on what's important to you, and act as an oath or vow renewal. It does not have to involve anyone else, be that gods, spirits, or humans. However, you can call them as witnesses to your ritual.

Lunar Schedule: Shortly after the new moon, when the waxing crescent moon is in the sky. This is a good time for new beginnings.

Time of Day: Evening, preferably when you have two to three hours alone and can go to sleep afterward.

Supplies
Bless/consecrate the following items before your ritual:
- An oil for anointing (Can be a special blend, a favorite essential oil, or simply olive oil poured in a little bowl)
- A white candle, holder, and matches
- An outfit/jewelry that inspires and works for wherever you plan to do you ritual (indoors or out)

Preparations
Eat lightly. Take a cleansing bath or shower, dress in your chosen attire, and have the oil and candle ready. Head to your chosen location (in front of your altar, a mirror, or perhaps a favorite spot in nature).

The Ritual
Perform the 3 Breaths exercise.

Create magical space in the style of your choosing.

Light the candle and say:

May the path before this Witch be illuminated and the shadows known.

Taking the oil, anoint yourself as follows:
As you anoint each breast to represent the Witch Lungs, say:

May my breath connect with the world.

Anoint the sternum for the Witch Heart, saying:

May my heart guide me true.

Anoint the navel/belly for the Serpent, saying:

May the words I speak be rooted in the power of truth.

Anoint the hands and feet for the Witch Bones, saying:

May the work I do honor and inspire the world.

Anoint the forehead for the Weaver, saying:

May my mind accept wisdom and be open to learn always.

Standing with feet and arms outstretched, say:

*I seek to connect the threads and weave my magic in the world. As I stand
in this place, in the presence of the sacred, I declare that my body, my blood,
my spirit, are that of the Witch. From this day forth, this Witch is known.*

Take a few moments to listen and feel around you, noting any changes or visions. When ready, open the space and prepare for bed. Record your dreams in the morning.

Ultimately, the best rituals are the ones you create yourself, so consider this a guideline for inspiration. Feel free to embellish it if you're so inspired.

Witch Anatomy Sigil

You have journeyed through the five sigils of the magical body, interacting and reflecting upon each one. You can, of course, go back and work with any of the individual sigils at any time. When you feel you are ready, here is the final sigil that connects them all together: the Witch Anatomy Sigil. It is pictured here alongside the Sigil of the Weaver, Witch Lungs Sigil, Witch Heart Sigil, Witch Bones Sigil, and Serpent Sigil (at right, from top to bottom). Study the individual sigils and find the key components that make up the larger sigil. To work with this sigil, you can carve or draw it onto a large candle to place on your altar as a reminder of your Witch anatomy.

A little more difficult but quite powerful to do is to draw the sigil on your own body (with blessed oil via fingertip or with a makeup marker), starting at the base of your neck and continuing down to below your navel. This can be done as part of the dedication ritual above or with one of the movement meditations or exercises earlier in this book, or you can incorporate it into a ritual of your own creation.

Witch Anatomy Sigil

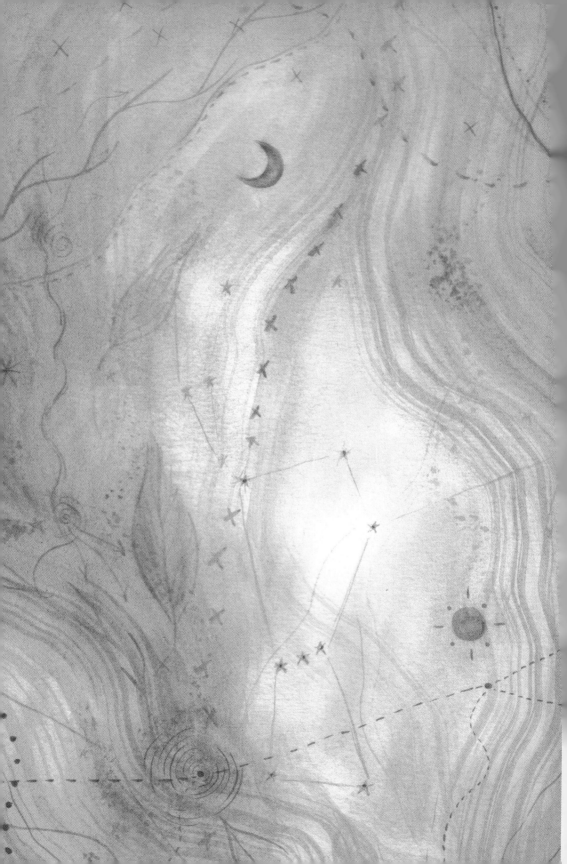

In Conclusion

As I finished writing the first draft of this very book, I happened upon a book sitting on the shelf of our local occult library. The title jumped out at me, but I had never heard of it and wasn't sure what to make of it from the back-cover description. I flipped it open and landed directly on the chapter "The Return of Pan." Taking that as a sign, I signed out the book and took it home with me to read. While I don't agree with all of the authors' theories, I feel like I could have written the following paragraph myself—and hopefully I have gotten the crux of it across to you through this book:

> The older spiritual traditions disparaged the body and regarded all of its desires as obstacles to be overcome. However in reality, being in a human body is an unparalleled opportunity to have many and diverse learning experiences. Spirituality is not about escaping the body and its functions; it is about embracing our total reality. To come into balance, we need to integrate the primal aspects of our nature, not reject them. To become gods, we need to know ourselves fully in body, mind and emotions, and rediscover ourselves in spirit.
>
> —David Ash and Peter Hewitt, *Science of the Gods: Reconciling Mystery & Matter* (Bath, UK: Gateway Books, 1991), 181

Be the Witch I know you are.

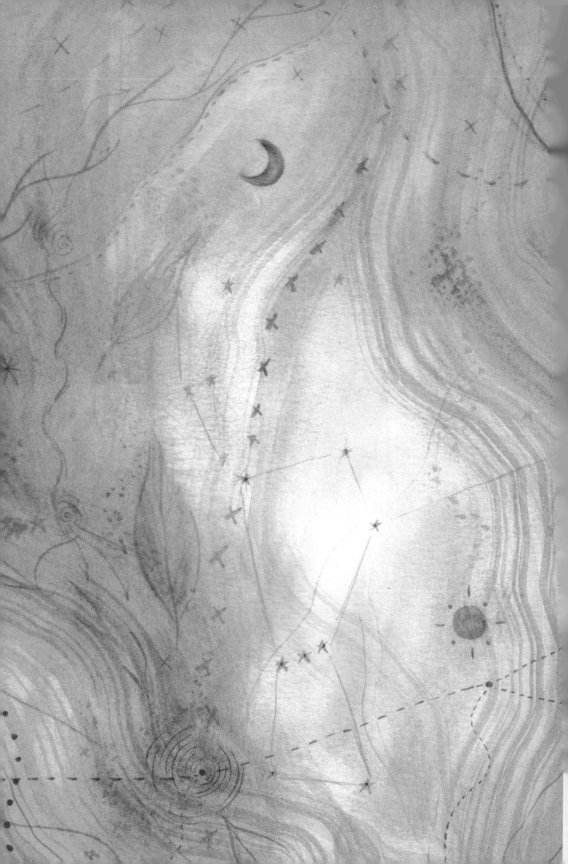

Acknowledgments

Much gratitude to my amazing friend and editor extraordinaire Elysia Gallo, whom I often hear in my head while I'm working on a book, so you can count that among her many superpowers. Much appreciation to Andrea Neff, whose editorial eye is constantly pushing my work to the next level with every book. Thank you to my mom, Terry Zakroff, for proofreading the second draft in record time. Big thanks to my test readers, Nova, Zeeke, Ivy, Rick, Shakira, Kelden, and Laura—your feedback was so helpful in fine-tuning this book. Thank you to my Patreon supporters, especially those who participated in our weekly Zoom sessions throughout the COVID-19 pandemic. Your enthusiasm, appreciation, and feedback helped create a semblance of sanity. For truly, what is time? Big technology jazz hands to Misha and Megan for elevating my book-writing software experience. Much love as always to my wonderful partner, Nathan—you always move me.

Bibliography

Ash, David, and Peter Hewitt. *Science of the Gods: Reconciling Mystery & Matter.* Bath, UK: Gateway Books, 1991.

Borreli, Lizette. "Can An Organ Transplant Change A Recipient's Personality? Cell Memory Theory Affirms 'Yes.'" Medical Daily. July 9, 2013. https://www.medicaldaily.com/can-organ-transplant-change-recipients-personality-cell-memory-theory-affirms-yes-247498.

Buckland, Raymond. *Buckland's Complete Book of Witchcraft.* St. Paul, MN: Llewellyn, 1986.

EurekAlert! "Dark 'Noodles' May Lurk in the Milky Way." American Association for the Advancement of Science (AAAS). January 21, 2016. https://www.eurekalert.org/pub_releases/2016-01/ca-dm011416.php.

Gary, Gemma. *Traditional Witchcraft: A Cornish Book of Ways.* London: Troy Books, 2019.

Gray, Eden. *Mastering the Tarot: Basic Lessons in an Ancient, Mystic Art.* New York: Crown, 1975.

Hersher, Rebecca. "The Making of Emotions, from Pleasurable Fear to Bittersweet Relief." NPR. June 1, 2017. https://www.npr.org/sections/health-shots/2017/06/01/530103479/the-making-of-emotions-from-pleasurable-fear-to-bittersweet-relief.

Huxley, Francis. *The Eye: The Seer and the Seen.* New York: Thames & Hudson, 1990.

K, Amber. *True Magick: A Beginner's Guide.* St Paul, MN: Llewellyn, 1990.

Klesman, Alison. "Galaxies Are Locked in Place by Their Surroundings." *Astronomy.* June 13, 2017. https://astronomy.com/news/2017/06/galaxy -cluster-alignment.

Koudounaris, Paul. *Heavenly Bodies: Cult Treasures & Spectacular Saints from the Catacombs.* New York: Thames & Hudson, 2013.

Laurie, Erynn Rowan. "The Cauldron of Poesy." The Preserving Shrine: Erynn Rowan Laurie. Accessed February 16, 2021. https://www.seanet .com/~inisglas/cauldronpoesy.html.

Lynch, Mary Pat. "The Three Cauldrons of Poesy: Dreams, Visions and Ancestry." Lecture presented at the IASD Conference, Montreal, 2008. http://www.threecauldrons.com/writing/written/ThreeCauldrons Montreal08MPL.pdf.

Maloney, Clarence, ed. *The Evil Eye.* New York: Columbia University Press, 1976.

Mathiesen, Robert and Theitic. *The Rede of the Wiccae: Adriana Porter, Gwen Thompson, and the Birth of a Tradition of Witchcraft.* Providence, RI: Olympian Press, 2005.

Michelle, Heron. "The Paradox of Personal Sovereignty in Modern Witchcraft." *Witch on Fire* (blog). *Patheos*, March 19, 2018. https://www.patheos.com /blogs/witchonfire/2018/03/paradox-personal-sovereignty/.

Pratchett, Terry. *Pyramids: The Book of Going Forth.* A Discworld novel. London: Corgi Books, 1990.

Turner, Victor W. "Symbols in African Ritual." *Science* 179, no. 4078 (March 16, 1973): 1100–1105. Accessed February 16, 2021. http://www.jstor.org/stable /1734971.

Wosien, Maria-Gabriele. *Sacred Dance: Encounter with the Gods.* New York: Avon Books, 1974.

Zakroff, Laura Tempest. *Weave the Liminal: Living Modern Traditional Witchcraft.* Woodbury, MN: Llewellyn, 2019.

———. *The Witch's Cauldron: The Craft, Lore & Magick of Ritual Vessels.* Woodbury, MN: Llewellyn, 2017.

Resources

I always like to include some interesting reading suggestions to keep your path full of inspiration.

For Fostering a Creative Mind (A Key Element for Magical Practice)

Art & Fear: Observations on the Perils (and Rewards) of Artmaking by David Bayles and Ted Orland

Ascending Pecularity: Edward Gorey on Edward Gorey edited by Karen Wilkin

Big Magic: Creative Living Beyond Fear by Elizabeth Gilbert

The Hearing Trumpet by Leonora Carrington

The Honey Month by Amal El-Mohtar

Magical Writing Grimoire: Use the Word as Your Wand for Magic, Manifestation & Ritual by Lisa Marie Basile

Making Magic: Weaving Together the Everyday and the Extraordinary by Briana Saussy

The Trickster's Hat: A Mischievous Apprenticeship in Creativity by Nick Bantock

For Strengthening Your Metaphysical Muscles—Mind, Body & Spirit

Braiding Sweetgrass: Indigenous Wisdom, Scientific Knowledge, and the Teachings of Plants by Robin Wall Kimmerer

The Four Elements of the Wise: Working with the Magickal Powers of Earth, Air, Water, Fire by Ivo Dominguez, Jr.

Honoring Your Ancestors: A Guide to Ancestral Veneration by Mallorie Vaudoise

The Magick of Food: Rituals, Offerings & Why We Eat Together by Gwion Raven

Outside the Charmed Circle: Exploring Gender & Sexuality in Magical Practice by Misha Magdalene

Practical Astrology for Witches and Pagans: Using the Planets and the Stars for Effective Spellwork, Rituals, and Magickal Work by Ivo Dominguez Jr.

Psychic Witch: A Metaphysical Guide to Meditation, Magick & Manifestation by Mat Auryn

Six Ways: Approaches & Entries for Practical Magic by Aidan Wachter

The Tradition of Household Spirits: Ancestral Lore and Practices by Claude Lecouteux

To Write to the Author

If you wish to contact the author or would like more information about this book, please write to the author in care of Llewellyn Worldwide Ltd. and we will forward your request. Both the author and the publisher appreciate hearing from you and learning of your enjoyment of this book and how it has helped you. Llewellyn Worldwide Ltd. cannot guarantee that every letter written to the author can be answered, but all will be forwarded. Please write to:

Laura Tempest Zakroff
℅ Llewellyn Worldwide
2143 Wooddale Drive
Woodbury, MN 55125-2989

Please enclose a self-addressed stamped envelope for reply,
or $1.00 to cover costs. If outside the U.S.A., enclose
an international postal reply coupon.

Many of Llewellyn's authors have websites with additional information and resources. For more information, please visit our website at http://www.llewellyn.com.

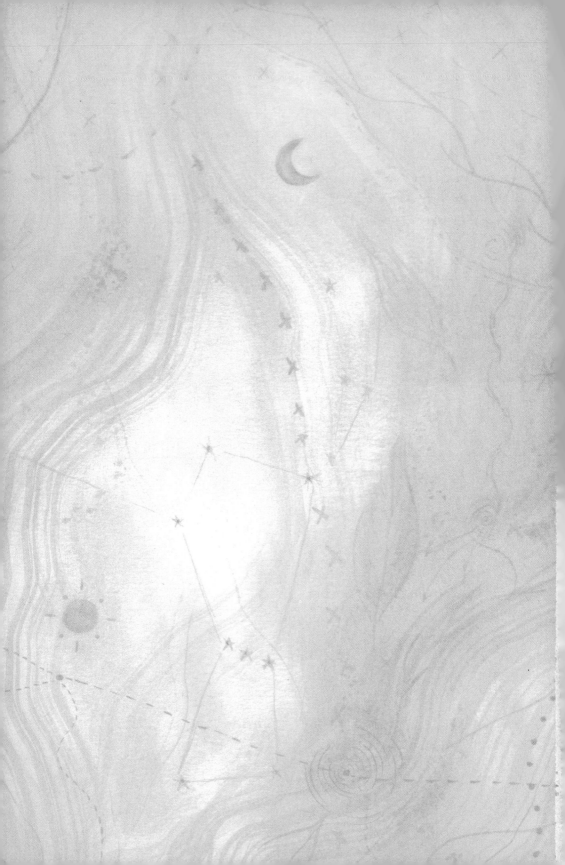